# The Seventh Inning Sit

## A JOURNEY OF ADHD

### Karen Lowry

ISBN: 1-4392-0822-0
ISBN-13: 9781439208229

Visit www.booksurge.com to order additional copies.

## DEDICATION

I dedicate this book to my husband, Vince, who gave me the inspiration to realize that this journey of advocacy needed to be written in order for others with children with ADHD to feel the need to be confident and courageous as they insure that their children's needs, both academic and emotional, are fully met. I also dedicate this book to our son, Jonathan, who as part of an intolerant world who believes ADHD must be seen to exist, will hopefully teach them someday that with all of their difficulties in fitting in to the "round peg," they possess gifts that others do not and inspire all of us who love them with all our heart.

# ACKNOWLEDGEMENTS

Throughout this journey, I have had the honor of working with three professionals who greatly contributed to the successful advocacy of Jon's needs in the area of academics and social skills. I must thank Dr. Louis Pica,Jr., a psychologist from Haddon Township, NJ, who always has served to boost a sagging self-esteem. The educating of the public school about the use of positive behavioral plans helped Jon to better function in an otherwise unaccepting environment during the course of 4th grade.

Thank you to Dr. Jackie Hoffman, a learning consultant and advocate who has her office in Moorestown,NJ. She was the first person to correctly evaluate testing results and to confirm a language-based learning disability. She has been by my side, supporting me in my quest of advocacy.

And finally, a thank you to Dr. Richard Selznic, psychologist, director of The Cooper Learning Center in Voorhees, NJ, and author of the excellent book, The Shut-Down Learner. When Jon was in second grade, he confirmed that Jon was dyslexic and needed research-based programs to learn to read. Since the writing of this book, he has administered a psycho-educational exam that has shown that the public school had indeed "left him behind."

As a result of his expertise and that of the previous two providers, the public school system had no choice but to grant out-of-district placement where he has begun to thrive. He has begun to learn compensatory skills that will serve him well as he learns to deal with ADHD and learning differences. Most importantly, he will develop a healthy self-esteem and beable to advocate for his needs as he moves through the school system and on into college. Having the ability to read and to learn impacts self-esteem. As far as I am concerned, without a positive self-esteem, there is no success.

Many of us make resolutions that we cannot keep. It was January 1996. I had three beautiful children. Megan was fourteen, Justin was nine, and Meredith was seven. It was the first year that I had all three children in school full-time. Of course, I had been, and would continue to be, a volunteer in the school. I also helped with homework, transported children to a multitude of events, and planned to continue in Girl Scouts in whatever capacity was needed. The multi-tasking does not end for a mom. But I felt at a loss.

Long ago, my husband and I had decided that, if it were possible, I would be a stay at home mom. Long before my marriage and children, I had gone to school to become a registered nurse. I initially worked on an adult floor of a Philadelphia center city hospital, but I soon decided that I wanted to deal with sick children and their families. I found myself at Children's Hospital of Philadelphia working in an acute care unit. It was difficult to not become attached to kids who were either acutely ill or tragically injured. In dealing with their families, I prided myself on the ability to be empathetic to the sometimes horrific situations in which they found themselves. Not only was it important to be empathetic, but it also was necessary to be there for the rights of the children, children who could not always speak for themselves.

I remember one night when a two-year-old child came into our unit after a car accident in New Jersey. Her mom was the driver and had been rushed to a local hospital. This child appeared to be in such critical condition that she was flown to us. She was on a ventilator with several life-saving tubes coming out of her, necessary to infuse drugs that could possibly save her. A monitoring device was placed in her head, a device that measured brain pressure, an indicator of the degree of brain swelling.

A multitude of physicians were around her, some of them neurosurgeons. They continued to yell out orders to the resident on call, who in turn would shout them out to us. Eventually, anyone with any experience in critical care realized that this little child was brain dead. It was obvious that the neurosurgeons believed this too by the level of experimentation going on within their orders. The resident physician on-call continued to carry out the orders and added some experimentation of his own. The other nurse continued to listen and follow through.

From my point of view, the line had been crossed. Behaviors delineated to save a life transformed into behaviors of experimentation, testing out drugs and reactions…the respect of this human life was gone. I refused to continue following orders on this little child's behalf and also on behalf of the injured mom, who was on her way in to see her child. Everyone became motionless and then physically backed away from the toddler's bed.

The other nurse was angry with me and could not believe that I would refuse orders. But I believed the toddler needed to be presentable for her mom…who needed to hold her and deal with this tragedy.

A priest was called who spoke with the mom at length. She was given the option to hold her child. She refused. It would have been better for her if she had been able to say good-bye, but she could not. At least I know that the care her child received did not consist of selfish, self-motivating behaviors.

We expect those who are professionals in any area of expertise to know best. That is not always the case, as I would later find out in my own personal life. As I began to set up job interviews since my youngest was now in school full-time, I began to anticipate a different role in life. Not that I would not continue to believe that being a good mom was the most important role that I had, but I wanted to also go back to another past role, being a registered nurse.

On the morning of my first job interview, I awoke and was completely stunned. I knew that I was pregnant. Five pregnancy tests later, my husband and I, although still in shock, began to accept the shock. After the obstetric appointment, we were aware that life would once again change for us.

It was an uneventful pregnancy. I was forty-two years old. Of course, I was worried about all the things that could go wrong, but I was determined that no invasive tests would occur that would jeopardize this little life. Whatever happened, we would accept it. I continued to run, take care of my other children, and remain positive.

On December 26, 1996, I delivered a nine-pound, fifteen-ounce baby boy via C-section. He was beautiful and healthy. We were ecstatic!

## EARLY INDICATIONS

When Jonathan was two, something occurred that made me wonder about his development. Since he was my only child at home, I wanted to do all the "mommy and me" things. I took him to a mommy and me music program where other moms and their toddlers met in a group and explored singing and playing with instruments that would make noise. Jonathan never really took to the program. He would rarely participate and would rather walk away and explore his environment.

After one session, I decided that since a mommy and me gathering was supposed to foster a nurturing relationship between child and parent, and since it was doing anything but that, I would not return. Continuing to want to strive to be mom of the year to my little precious toddler, I looked for other avenues of adventure. I decided to take him to a local bookstore to listen to a story and then do a craft with other children. Since his siblings were so much older, this would give Jonathan a chance to interact with his peers, as well as make me feel that I was bonding to him.

As soon as we walked into the bookstore and approached the group, Jonathan froze and started to cry. He made it very clear to me that what I was planning for him did not fit into his plans. No amount of coaxing changed his behavior. I decided reluctantly to leave.

At the time I was confused and sad. But I know now that Jonathan was sending me a message that I would later understand.

Jonathan entered kindergarten at a local Catholic school. I was so happy for him. His teacher, Mrs. E, had been teaching for quite some time. She seemed never to tire of these very active and at times mischievous children. Her classroom every year had a theme. This year, much to Jonathan's delight, the theme was the railroad. He absolutely loved trains. It was a classroom of round desks, with different stations all over the room. The children were encouraged to move from station to station during certain periods of the day to experience different activities, whether it be computers, books, or toys that would encourage interaction.

Being one of two homeroom moms, I was in the classroom quite often. At that age, there were numerous events that required parental involvement. As a result, I was well aware of Jonathan's behavior.

Along with direct communication with Mrs. E, we also had a log that would allow communication whenever there were any problems. This was initiated as a result of some behavior that had started and which had become disruptive to the class. If the day was good for Jonathan, he was given a smiley face in the log for that day. If the day was not good, he was given a sad face for the day. His motivation to behave was supposed to come from the desire to receive a special treat at the end of the week. Also, the thought was that, at his age, he wanted to please the significant adults in his life, such as his parents and his teacher. So why, you might ask, would it be a problem for behavior to be acceptable?? The answer to that question would not be evident for a while.

The focus on whether or not it was a good day was not related to academics but to behavior. Jonathan always called out rather than raise his hand as directed. He would interrupt other children as well as the teacher. Many times he refused to do what was asked of him. For instance, if they were in a circle on the floor listening to Mrs. E play her guitar and sing, he would either get up and walk around looking at things around the room and outside the window, or he would lie on the floor while in the circle, disturbing others around him by getting in their personal space.

A child soon becomes the "bad kid" in the eyes of his peers when he is always getting corrected for some behavior. He then becomes angry and even more oppositional. If there were any disagreements in the class, Jonathan was always blamed.

I had known before he was two that Jonathan "marched to another drummer" as his kindergarten teacher stated to me. She and I spoke and decided that maybe it was time to consider having him tested for ADHD. I called Children's Hospital of Philadelphia in the spring of his kindergarten year, 2002. Most unfortunately, somehow Jonathan and I fell through cracks and the appointment that was to be in the summer of 2002 was not scheduled. So his evaluation did not take place until September. He would start first grade without his ducks in order and without his new teacher understanding what was necessary to help him succeed.

On the second day of first grade, I decided that it would be important to go into the school and introduce myself to Jonathan's teacher. If she was frustrated with his behavior, she would at least know the child's mom and also know that I understood, that I supported her, and that he would be tested later that month. I believed, based on human nature, that her frustration with my son would be alleviated by my attempts to be available and supportive. I hoped to present myself as an involved parent trying to do the right thing, which equated, hopefully, to more tolerance for this small, impulsive boy whose behavior at times would be unacceptable in her classroom.

I rushed to the school and then to his classroom. The class was just coming back from an activity. As the class filed into their room, I reached out my hand to the teacher, introducing myself as Jonathan's mom. Her response was my worst nightmare. Ms. A never reached out her hand to me to introduce herself. She gave me the feeling that, on this second day of school, she would have been happier if this child were elsewhere. She merely stated, "Kind of busy…"

I looked over at my son to see a somewhat disheveled looking child, his shirt un-tucked, his hair tousled, as he marched into the classroom close behind the child in front of him.

Even though my introduction had been ignored, I decided then to briefly reassure the teacher that a plan for Jonathan was in place. I was starting to realize how typical it is to feel embarrassed and apologetic when discussing your child with ADHD characteristics, especially with someone who was seemingly intolerant.

I told this teacher that within a couple of weeks I would be taking Jonathan to Children's Hospital for evaluations. Fortunately, his kindergarten teacher had explained to her a little bit about what he was like and some positive actions to take, like placing him in front of the class to encourage more focus and on-task behavior. She agreed and looked forward to learning about the outcome of the tests. I assured her that I would keep her informed.

# EVALUATION FOR ADHD

Jonathan was evaluated and diagnosed with ADHD by the end of September 2003, at the beginning of first grade. Unfortunately, there is not a test that can concretely visualize ADHD. It is based on interview methods that involve the teacher, the parent, and if appropriate, the child. A good medical history and physical are important to rule out any other issues that could look like ADHD. That's why it is so important to go to an experienced developmental pediatrician who has expertise in ADHD. Of course, other professionals may diagnose ADHD, like psychologists and psychiatrists. Most important is that they have a level of expertise in the process of diagnosing ADHD. Symptoms of ADHD in children are behaviors that can be a part of any child. But the difference is that the symptoms occur more frequently, with more acuity, and affect the success in at least two areas of life. For instance, the child appears to be affected negatively socially and academically. It was recommended that behavior modification and medication be used as they would be advantageous in helping to control his symptoms of ADHD. In addition to this diagnosis, we were told that he exhibited signs of learning disabilities in the areas of reading. Because of the letter reversals, lack of decoding skills, and the difficulty with letter recognition Jonathan exhibited, it was recommended by The Children's Hospital of Philadelphia that he receive a full child study team evaluation to accurately assess the presence of a learning disability. They could not do that there, as they are a medical facility. ADHD is a medical diagnosis. School districts have child study teams that consist of social workers, psychologists, and case managers who have some expertise in learning disorders. So discovery of a learning disability would have to be handled by those in education. It is important to remember that ADHD is a medical diagnosis and a learning disability is an educational diagnosis. No one in education has the credentials to diagnose ADHD.

In addition, it was concluded that Jonathan also had oppositional defiant disorder, which simply was a word that encompassed his non-compliant and argumentative behaviors. The diagnosis of ADHD has a high percentage of co-existing disorders that include learning disabilities and oppositional defiant disorder as I would later find out. In addition, it was felt that Jon was at risk for anxiety disorder, another affliction that does occur in kids with ADHD.

## THE MEDICATION DEBATE

My husband and I were horrified. We absolutely did not want to put Jonathan on any medication. Somehow, at the time, it sounded as if putting him on any meds would only serve to alter his personality and maybe even put his present and future health at risk. We were told that there were actually physiological differences in function between a child who did not have ADHD and a child who did. My son's frontal lobe was actually UNDERACTIVE, meaning he was therefore unable to control his impulsivity like kids whose frontal lobe functioned properly. Medications like Ritalin and Concerta were actually stimulants that would allow him to be less impulsive and to focus more on school work.

We left Children's Hospital feeling frustrated, sad, and angry…the gamut of emotions experienced by parents who have just been told that their precious child is less than perfect. We both decided that we would give it time and not make any decisions regarding medications right away. And as the journey would move on, we would learn that this diagnosis did not alter his perfection. It would just mean that Jon would (with our help) have to learn how to succeed in school where he was expected to fit into their round pegs, despite the fact that he functioned as a square one!

In order to ensure enough academic help, it appeared that we would have to have Jonathan tested by a child study team through the school. Both his teacher and principal were aware now of his diagnosis and had already been concerned about learning issues. So testing was set up through County Special Services. Testing would take several days because first, we did not want him to miss a lot of class time, and second, he could not effectively focus for greater than a fifteen to twenty minute period.

During this period of testing, which was in November, Jonathan showed more and more signs of impulsivity. His teacher was exasperated and would call me complaining that Jonathan would not sit down throughout the course of a day. Instead he would wander around, gaze out the window, and not only be on the wrong page of a lesson, but be in the wrong book!!

For example, during a math lesson, teams were formed, and each team had to answer math facts using flash cards. All of this excitement appeared to make Jonathan more impulsive so that he was blurting out incorrect answers and answering late because of not focusing on the current questions.

After this activity, everyone was told to go back to their seats and take out their math books. Jonathan stood at his desk, yelling out the incorrect page to turn to in the book. The children were annoyed and told him to sit down. As the class was directed to each problem, Jonathan rushed through them inaccurately, flipping rapidly through his book. He not only was not following along during the lesson but he was a major distraction to the rest of the class.

I would later find out from reading about ADHD, that environment can certainly play a role in behavior. With an increase in confusion and activity can come more hyperactivity and impulsive behavior. Certainly, playing a highly charged interactive competitive game would stimulate all of the characteristics of ADHD, thereby increasing both impulsivity and behavior that was not focused.

Shortly after Jonathan was tested at CHOP, I consulted with the first of many educational professionals about ADHD, wanting to use behavior techniques to help him. This educator…and apparent expert in ADHD…was very obviously stunned and horrified at my husband's and my decision to not medicate. She was very frank, and at this early stage of acceptance of ADHD, an entity that I still did not clearly understand, I was unable to deal with her and that bluntness. She told me that if I really thought that I was going to actually make changes in Jonathan's behavior without the use of medication, I was very wrong.

In the world of health care, when parents are told that their child is terminally ill or possibly won't survive an accident, there are several stages that they must go through before any acceptance is to take place. They are sad and angry, they may try to bargain with God, they may try to gather more facts or opinions, or just plain denial may be evident. While I certainly won't compare the death of a child to a diagnosis of ADHD, a parent still is in a similar position, one of absolutely having to accept the diagnosis before that parent can be of any value to that child.

When I went to that learning consultant, I was sad and wanted to deny the necessity of half of the therapy that was recommended to me by CHOP; only behavior modification was necessary for him, I decided. This teacher would not accept my belief that medication could be deleted in the plan of treatment. But because of the stage I was in, which was denial, I would not believe that medication was a necessity. Also, I felt that I was still in the process of gathering information in order to make an informed and intelligent decision that would significantly impact my child. I left her office angry and determined that I was not going to drug my child!!

Meanwhile, as Christmas break approached, things in Jonathan's classroom were not getting any easier. He continued to yell out, look out the window, walk around without permission creating chaos, getting in children's personal space by pushing, butting in line, not taking turns, and just plain being oppositional.

In addition, because of all of these characteristics of ADHD, Jon was also not successful in the academic arena. CHOP had previously indicated the possibility of a learning disability. Certainly, an ability to focus is crucial to learning, especially when dealing with a learning disability.

I began to realize that maybe we needed to re-consider medicating him. My husband agreed. So began the very frustrating process of determining the correct dosage. Unlike other pediatric medications whose dosages are based on weight, the dosages with these stimulants are based on trial and error. Typically a small dose is started. Then it is necessary for the educational system to evaluate behaviors through the week using a rating scale. This rating scale evaluates behaviors and levels of focus by having teachers assign numbers ranging from one to four, with one being "never" to four being "always."

This is a time of helplessness for parents. You want what's best for your child and you want to evaluate it yourself, but the evaluation must take place during school when you can't be there. And many times, by the time your child comes home, at least in the case of Jonathan, the medication has been metabolized and is therefore no longer effective. Some medications require a blood level for adequate effectiveness. In the case of a stimulant, once it is metabolized, it is no longer in the body. Besides, even if there is any functioning medication left in his system, he is no longer in the environment where he so desperately needs to focus and behave. So the parent is not in the position to evaluate the effectiveness of the dosage. It is imperative for the teacher to use the rating scales to objectively describe behaviors that the medication is supposed to help. Those behaviors would include both impulsive, hyperactive behaviors as well as the ability to stay focused and on task.

As another side note to the above: Sometimes parents who advocate for their child are looked upon as annoying and stressed. In my experience, sometimes teachers will take it upon themselves to attempt methods that they consider calming to the parent. Presumably, a stressed out parent does create "waves." Many times after a drug dosage change, I have asked his teacher how he is doing. The response is always positive. He is doing great and is improving. On one such occasion that occurred, I then sent in the behavior checklists to hopefully better evaluate the effectiveness of the medication. The response I got was not what I would consider "great." That tool absolutely showed information crucial to dosage adjustment. Once a teacher was given a tool where she had to rate behaviors, it then became clear as to how Jon was really doing.

## DEVELOPING AN IEP

The child study team from the County Special Services completed the evaluations and was ready to give us the results by the beginning of December. In addition to having ADHD, Jonathan also showed indicators of a language-based learning disability. Apparently, according to the experts, a very high percentage of children with ADHD do indeed have a learning disability. Test scores indicated that Jonathan had difficulties in listening comprehension and vocabulary, and that he had weak auditory processing skills.

Under the educational laws of the state, Jon would be classified with ADHD and a language -based learning disability that would make him eligible for special education services. This would of course be another reason that made it so necessary for Jonathan to be able to focus.

It was now time to develop a plan to help Jon with his different way of learning. The child study team, comprised of a case manager, his classroom teacher, the principal, a speech and language teacher, a special education teacher, and a basic skills teacher, now began developing his ISP, his individual support plan. This was similar to an IEP, an individual education plan. This consisted of pulling him out of the class for extra help in reading and speech.

This new plan would not take place until after the holidays, although we met on December 17, 2003, to put the plan in place. In the area of reading, Jonathan would receive supplemental instruction in reading twice a week for thirty minutes in a small group. He would also be pulled out of class once a week for twenty minutes for speech services to work on articulation problems. He had difficulties with the correct pronunciation of "r" and "l."

So in January 2004, Jonathan would be serviced with extra help that would hopefully keep him up with his peers. Through feedback from his teacher using rating scales, Jonathan seemed to be doing better in the areas of impulsivity and focus ability. I was sure that the extra help was at least giving him some sense of success, reducing his anxiety to some degree.

Although things seemed better, I remained very vigilant and concerned. I asked for an ISP meeting about four weeks into the beginning of the institution of his new educational plan. I was told that it was too soon and that waiting another month would better evaluate his progress. I reluctantly agreed. From my point of view, Jonathan was still very difficult at home. By the time he got home, the Adderall, the current stimulant that he was on, was fully metabolized. Doing homework was very difficult due to his lack of focus and oppositional behavior.

Although the experts say that oppositional behavior is highly correlated with ADHD, I had to wonder why. In my heart I knew that this very difficult behavior had to be at least partially the result of a lot of frustration, loneliness, low self-esteem, and anger. Frustration because of his difficulty with work and inability to stay focused all of the time, loneliness because of a perceived feeling that no one understood what was going on in his head, low self-esteem because he knew that he was not like everyone else, and anger because he did not want to be all of the above.

## MOUNTING CONCERN

So the child study team meeting occurred in March 2004. All participating parties were present; his teacher, his special education teacher, his basic skills teacher, his speech teacher, his case manager, and the principal. They continued to say that they felt Jonathan was doing fine. His medication and the extra help were contributing to his success.

Although they were the experts, I had so many doubts. I told them that I was concerned about his reading and comprehension. I believed that any reading that was observed was based on memorization. The whole team in unison yelled out all at once: "This is how a child learns to read!" I said that I was aware of that, but I did not feel at this point that the rule of memorization applied. His first-grade teacher patted me on the head and told me that I needed to calm down. One of many frustrating moments on this very long journey, I would find out.

## A REASON FOR CONCERN FROM A SPEECH AND LANGUAGE THERAPIST

I decided to continue speech and language therapy through the summer so that Jonathan would not at least fall backwards. I took him to a speech and language pathologist for assessment and intervention. It worried me that his articulation difficulties seemed to take priority during his school interventions while another very large picture, processing and expression, was being left behind.

This speech pathologist was wonderful. Her name was Amy. Amy was a very warm and approachable teacher. Jonathan quickly knew that she was very accepting of his many struggles. She quickly assessed that he had significant comprehension and language processing difficulties. We decided together that this would be our focus, rather than giving our attention to difficulties in some sound formations since he was at least receiving this help at school. Because she saw that Jonathan had difficulty staying on task and complying with what was expected of him, she conducted the sessions within a structured environment. He knew what to expect and was rewarded with prizes and stickers when he accomplished goals. At times he would refuse to perform certain challenges. This would necessitate frequent breaks as well as consequences when he continued to refuse.

It was June 2004 when we started speech and language with Amy, the summer following first grade. He was assessed by her as being eight to ten months behind in comprehension. She felt that his lack of ability to concentrate related to ADHD and that it negatively impacted his ability to process language he read. She found that if the lesson was at least presented in a game format, he would attend more consistently. His thinking and reasoning were delayed, as well as his ability to remember facts and information needed to comprehend. His ability to comprehend was based on visual cues, reminders, repetition, and accentuating main ideas. Even then, his ability to grasp main ideas many times fell below fifty percent.

Jonathan also showed a significant lapse in his ability to express himself. Again I think that, although learning disabled, his ability to retrieve necessary language to tell a story or describe an event had a lot to do with his ADHD. His level of focus was not enough to provide that ability. And as I later learned, short term- memory is also affected in children with ADHD. And again, with that came low self-esteem followed by giving up.

## PRIVATE TESTING

In addition to having speech and language therapy throughout the summer of 2004, I decided that I wanted to have Jonathan tested privately. His testing by the County Special Services had been done at a time of great turmoil. We originally had decided not to allow medication. When behaviors were noted to be so disruptive that he had no focus ability at all, we decided at the time that we seemed to no longer have the choice. His impulsivity was affecting his social life, and his hyperactivity and inattentiveness were affecting his learning. But when we made this decision, it was half-way through the testing. Would scores have changed had he been tested on medication throughout the entire process? I set out on another journey of discovery.

On July 9, 2004, I took Jonathan to an educational consultant who had her own child study team. The educational assessment comprised of evaluating his writing skills, his reading comprehension, decoding of words, fluency, oral expression, and math skills. It was noted that although Jon had some skills in decoding, his comprehension was below average, as was his ability to orally express himself.

As a parent, it was very hard to put this child through so much testing. Once it is done, you expect the experts to be able to assess the data and come up with a diagnosis that will lend itself to the right kind and amount of remedial help. This is where I have grave concern for those of you who have set out in a journey such as ours; concern based on the level of trust we as parents give teaching professionals.

The following will give support to the need to always follow up on assessment of data from testing. A second opinion is always a good idea, especially if you feel strongly that something is being missed. I have learned that it is imperative to believe in yourself when you feel something is not being addressed. Be courageous and go forward to find all the complete answers to your child's struggles. Chances are that you will be surprised at your intuitiveness. I wish I had done this sooner, as you will see.

## A STARTLING RESPONSE IN AN IEP MEETING

We met with the school personnel and the child study team who originally tested Jonathan in September 2004, hoping to set up the right support for second grade. Present at this meeting were the principal, the new second-grade teacher, the math and reading support teachers, the speech teacher, the basic skills teacher, and the case manager. I presented to them the testing that was done in the summer. I explained that Jonathan was on Ritalin at the time of this testing.

After looking at the material, the case manager decided that Jonathan no longer needed reading support, only math support. I was stunned! She and the others present decided that there were enough values in the tests that would indicate that Jonathan was average and therefore did not need support. Despite my protests, they decided to pull Jonathan's reading support. I did not care how they came up with their beliefs…of course, they were the professionals in this area and I was only the parent.

I should have followed my instincts and taken this to a higher level. By this, I mean I wished that I had gone to the case manager's supervisor for a better evaluation of the test data. You know, sometimes it is so much easier to believe the positive you are told and not believe what is in your heart. This child study team was telling me that the data was showing that Jonathan did not need support. At least, how they were reading and interpreting the data indicated that his ability was average. I knew they were wrong, but I decided to give Jonathan a chance and continue to observe. After all, this test was done while he was on the medication. With more ability to focus, maybe he would be fine, I thought.

Late January and into February, my feelings of concern began to surface once again. Jonathan was not doing well in tests that required reading comprehension. His fluency while reading was poor. If it takes you twice as long to read a paragraph as others, by the time of completion can you expect to comprehend what you read? I think not.

## A PRIVATE EVALUATION; THE ANSWER TO A CONCERN

In the middle of February 2005, I took Jonathan to a learning center. No matter what teachers were telling me, I knew in my heart that my child was suffering. That proverbial shoe was going to eventually drop…Would I, a lay person in the world of educators, be able to stop it?

This journey that Jonathan and I were on necessitated another set of tests. The results that followed were stunning: He could read words in isolation, but as the words became more complex, he began to encounter much more difficulty. The tester, a licensed psychologist, school psychologist, and assistant clinical professor of pediatrics, saw that as words became more complex, Jonathan could not read them. He assessed Jon's ability to read the simple words as being related to visual memory; decoding ability was not occurring to decipher the more complex words.

As you might remember, it was in first grade that I expressed to the child study team my concern that Jon was appearing to read only because he was able to remember words that he had learned. At the time, I was told to calm down and that this was how children learn to read.

Further, Jonathan was asked to read a second grade passage. He read very laboriously and very slowly. Substitution errors occurred, which altered the meaning. The meaning was difficult enough due to the slow pace at which he was reading. He was then supposed to write an assignment. This writing passage was poorly organized with spelling errors throughout. This tester decided that Jon had a severe writing and spelling disability. In short, his evaluation showed a reading/learning disability consistent with dyslexia!

My emotions were so scattered. I was upset, disappointed, and scared that my child had a learning disability that was affecting his ability to read and comprehend. Yet my journey was finally making some sense. In my heart, I knew that the school personnel were missing the educational diagnosis. The medical diagnosis of ADHD was already in place. But the co-existing condition of dyslexia was somehow not acknowledged by the educational professionals, despite all of the testing. They certainly were not interested in any assessments that I, a mere mom, would make. Now I had a professional who documented what I had truly known all along. My child needed special remediation for a decoding problem in order to read fully and be able to comprehend.

## CLASHING OF OPINIONS

A couple of weeks later, after the diagnosis and after I decided to place him in a private reading program three hours a week, his teacher and a basic skills teacher asked to have a meeting with me. They said that Jonathan was unable to comprehend and handed me a book to help him. I told them that what was happening was an inability to decode and hence to read. Being unable to decode words means not only lack of fluency but lack of comprehension.

The teachers still believed that it was only a comprehension problem. I insisted that they were wrong and told them that he was now officially diagnosed with dyslexia and that I had enrolled him in a reading program. They seemed stunned. Sometimes I think being too proactive as a parent can be somewhat intimidating. That's the feeling I got from them anyway.

## THE DEVASTATING LIE

As Jonathan's second-grade year was progressing to an end, I found myself with a son who had no self-esteem and was continuing to fail. Toward the end of May, I called an ISP meeting to go over the year and hopefully make changes to his support. After reviewing materials like current grades and the new evaluation of Jonathan that diagnosed him as dyslexic, the case manager casually mentioned that perhaps we needed to put back the reading support that had been pulled at the beginning of the year.

I could not believe how casual and matter-of-fact she was as she said it. I was stunned...but not as stunned as when she then said, "Well, you never wanted this support anyway."

You could have heard a pin drop. Her devastating lie seemed to bounce off all of the walls and vibrate in my head. I looked around at the professionals: his classroom teacher, his basic skills teacher, both reading and math specialists, his speech teacher, and principal. No one said a word except the basic skills teacher, who protested and said that what she said really was not accurate. No response came from anyone else. This same case manager had previously told me that this Catholic school was not obligated to follow the support plans in place the way the public schools did.

Again, I was stunned. Is that what you say to a mom who is obviously overwhelmed with concern for her son who is dyslexic with ADHD? So, as I tried to recover after this lie without support from most of the professionals in the room, I turned to the principal. After having been told by my case manager that this school did not actually have to follow these learning plans that we so painstakingly put together and that we talked about in these special meetings, I asked her what assurance she could give me that the third-grade teacher would follow the plan so that my son would thrive?? Of course, she was full of reassurance in her condescending way. She told me that there was one child in the current third grade who was classified with a learning disability and he was doing quite well.

Well, it scares me when a so-called teaching professional acts as if the category of learning disabled children consists of one type of child who needs one type of intervention. In addition, the diagnosis of ADHD only can complicate the classroom management of that learning disabled child. Along with the fact that Jon learns differently are all of the manifestations of ADHD: impulsivity, lack of focus, and restlessness. And these are surface symptoms. Without reading about ADHD, the teacher would not understand the forgetfulness, the disorganization, and the lack of working memory. This principal, in addition to placing learning disabled children into one category, failed to recognize the diagnosis of ADHD and how, at least in Jon's case, it would impact his learning.

## FACIAL TICS AND PLUMMETING SELF-ESTEEM

I had been involved with quite a few child study team meetings up to this point. None was as devastating as this one, especially coming on the heels of Jon's increasingly obvious difficulties with decoding, reading comprehension, and processing. The other heartbreaking piece was a kid who knew that he was failing. He began to develop facial tics. What I had learned about this co-existing condition was that kids with ADHD may have them. They are not caused by the stimulants used for focus, but these meds can certainly cause latent tics to come to the surface with obvious symptoms. These symptoms included facial muscle spasms, which in turn included the appearance of eye squinting. At times they were so bad that I am sure that Jon could not have complete vision.

We decided to take Jon off all medications for the summer. We felt that maybe if we gave him a break from stimulants, the tics would go away and he would be able to later tolerate another stimulant. Yes, this was definitely a layperson's perspective. But sometimes there are no clear cut answers to questions or solutions to problems. Sometimes it is important to make decisions based on what your heart is telling you. The developmental pediatrician said that we could try a different stimulant, but since all of the stimulants worked in the same way, chances were good that another one would have the same effect. But in my heart, although scientifically I believed all of this to be true, I knew something else. I knew that those latent tics were beginning to show their ugly head because of stress—a seven-year-old's perception that he was not doing well academically, that he was drowning. No one was saving him, certainly not his teachers.

In May of second grade, Jonathan had done poorly on a quiz. He went to his teacher and asked why he had done so badly. The response, "Well, next time do better." So a teacher was in essence telling him that he could control the fact of doing better. But in his heart he knew he could not. How does a child make sense of such a conflict between whether or not he has control over what he can read and comprehend? And how can he make sense out of the need to control his ability to focus when even he knows that he lacks that control? After all, adults (and especially teachers in this case) are supposed to be right. So why did it not feel right?? Ultimately, the outcome of this teacher's expectations was a continuing plummeting of self-esteem and the development of tics.

# EVALUATING PROGRAMS BEST SUITED FOR YOUR CHILD

I began to believe that I needed to again investigate the possibility that public school was really where Jon belonged. In the very beginning of first grade, I had sent all of his tests to the county director of special education services, who in turn said that he would have his child study team look at it and determine whether he was receiving adequate service in the catholic school. He came back to me and said that Jonathan was currently receiving the same amount of support that he would receive in public school. This director, I would later find out, also had a role in the amount of funds sent to the catholic school that would be earmarked for special education services.

Now, at the end of second grade, I knew something was terribly wrong. I visited with the principal of the public elementary school in our neighborhood. I knew him from the past since my two middle children had gone to that school. He, of course, walked the line, not wanting to insult the Catholic school and not wanting to overly compliment his school. But I wanted him to be real. I guess I wanted a professional in the field of teaching to give me honest answers and steer me in the right direction at this point in my journey. Although by now I certainly was aware of the most effective direction for Jon, I wanted confirmation from someone else at this point, a desire of mine. I finally asked him what he would do with a child who was diagnosed with dyslexia and ADHD, who was not at grade level in reading, and who was significantly below average in a standardized test taken among his peers.

Right before my eyes, he became real. He lost the façade. He looked directly into my eyes and said, "If I had a kid like that, I would transfer him to us immediately."

The following week, I was to bring Jonathan over to meet the principal and take a tour. I was very afraid. Kids with ADHD need structure and consistency. What would I be doing to his world by taking him out of a school he had been going to since he was four years old?

When I approached him on the idea of taking a tour of a new school, he seemed very intrigued by the thought. I was so surprised and thrilled. After the meeting and the tour, he immediately decided that he would like to transfer into the school for third grade. I had previously explained to him that he would receive more help and support. Despite the familiarity with his current school as well as his friends, he decided that going to the public school would be right for him. Sometimes children can truly amaze you. Sometimes they have far more insight than more mature and experienced adults.

From the time of Jonathan's ADHD diagnosis, I had been searching for information and professionals who could help. I had gone to a couple of learning consultants, but I did not feel right about them. As second grade came to an end and I knew of our fresh start ahead, I again went on a quest to find the right learning consultant, the right advocate, who could help us continue our journey and make it a successful one. I had advocated for my child all along to this point, and I would continue. But I wanted a partner, one who had the teaching expertise and knowledge of special education law. My quest was finally successful. I found someone who seemed like she had great credentials and experience. So I made the appointment. I went to Ms. Smith's office with all of my previous testing materials in hand. She would go over all of them in depth, but for now she briefly looked over the results. The confirmation of dyslexia was within the testing results. But I had never heard from any of the school professionals that any of the scores indicated this. As a matter of fact, these were the same test results that had prompted the previous case manager to withhold reading support. So again, the concern I had at the time was now validated! Again, this shows why it is so important to follow through in areas where in your heart you believe the professionals are incorrect.

Our journey now pointed out another flaw. Not only does a parent depend on those teachers to administer the correct tests, but the diagnosis is the outcome of correct assessment of the test results. You would expect this to be no problem. But I was finding out differently. The assessment of the data would need an expertise in the area of combining all results in each of the testing tools and then understanding what that all meant. Results taken out of context could give a totally different diagnosis.

I asked Ms. Smith why these tests were given when the testers seemed at times unable to figure out correctly what the scores meant. She said many were not educated in the areas of evaluating scores; that it was something one had to continually update as evaluation tools changed and became more difficult to utilize. So now I knew that Jonathan truly needed support that had not been available in the previous school.

The next appointment consisted of a meeting with Jonathan and Ms. Smith. She wanted to meet the child to fully understand the entire picture. She let him talk about himself and how he felt he was doing in school. At the end of the meeting, she understood that here was a child lacking self-esteem because he did not feel successful in the school where he had spent three years. She clearly saw a child who was willing to change his school environment and take on the task of meeting new friends in order to feel supported and successful. The goal by the end of the summer would be to meet with the child study team and ensure that a clear and appropriate IEP would be in place for third grade. That would mean an IEP (Individual Educational Plan) would be developed containing individual and measurable goals for Jon. There are a couple of differences between the previous ISP developed in the Catholic school and this IEP that was to be developed in public school. The IEP is a legal document and has to be followed by the school system. The ISP had neither characteristic.

## THE PREPARATION FOR PUBLIC SCHOOL

By August 2005, Ms. Smith, the case manager, and I met with previous testing material and previous IEP's from the catholic school. By then, Ms. Smith had fully read Jon's testing materials and had a good idea of what Jonathan was all about. The provisional plan was put in place. Jonathan would be pulled to a resource room twice a day for reading and math. He would also receive speech and language services twice a week.

## TIPS FOR MAINTAINING POSITIVE
## SCHOOL DAY STRUCTURE

In September when school started, Jon was very excited and nervous, as you would expect. We did start him back on medication so that he would be better able to focus. As studies have indicated, behavior is best controlled by medication and behavioral psychology. Behavioral psychology could encompass therapy with the child, therapy with the family, or the institution of a behavior plan both at home and at school. There are many kinds of behavior plans that can be used for reinforcing positive behavior. Since he spent about three hours of his day pulled out of the regular classroom in small resource room groups, it was important for those teachers, the resource room teacher and the speech and language teacher, to institute a behavior plan. It seemed that both of these special education teachers had an understanding of ADHD. They both seemed to have a behavior plan in place.

It is very important to kids with ADHD to have a positive plan that incorporates recognition of positive on-task behavior and does not emphasize negative behavior. A child with ADHD wants attention and, if he can get it, it really does not matter to him if the behavior that accomplished it was negative or positive. In a small setting, relationships form early. With Jon's strong and competitive personality as well as oppositional defiance, he would quickly become a leader whether anyone liked it or not! What worked for Jonathan was to be expected: Positive reinforcement for doing what was expected of him, rewards when goals were met, warnings before consequences. This was done using a card system. Things were good when his card was green…the card was changed to yellow (by him) when a warning was given. The warning would be related to such behaviors as talking to his peers, yelling out an answer without raising his hand, or any behavior that might contribute to him being off-task.

Any oppositional behavior would also necessitate a warning. If behavior did not improve after two warnings, then he would have to change his card to red, which meant a call home to me. Rewards included the ability to do activities that were considered to be a privilege, like erasing the board, taking things to the office, and being line leader. Important to this plan was Jon's input regarding acceptable rewards. He had to know what he was earning and he had to want it as well for the plan to be successful. He could also win coupons for prizes on a daily basis.

Rewards could not be delayed. Kids with ADHD need to know immediately that they are doing well. A similar reward system was in place in his speech class. The regular education class teacher did have some form of reward system, although it did not seem critical to Jonathan at the time. Behavior problems did not happen in the large class setting. But my concerns were not only related to impulsive behavior but also to areas of learning. I instituted a weekly progress report so that I could maintain contact consistently. I had found that in order to get objective information from teachers there is a need for some type of checklist or rating scale. Behaviors to be rated were as follows: respectful of adults, works well in cooperative groups, listens to and follows directions, makes good use of time, stays on task, and completes work on time. Each area was rated from one to four. One was never, two was rarely, three was sometimes, and four was often. There were many times that without this progress report, I would have missed out on knowing key information. When reports came home with low scores, I could follow up and discover the issues that created that low score.

Jonathan liked third grade, even though it was a challenge since he was behind significantly due to the lack of appropriate support at his previous school. But at least here at his new school, he felt supported and was being given the tools to catch up to his peers. I also think that Jonathan, despite his hyperactive and impulsive behavior, is a child who wants to please. His teacher was someone who he truly liked and looked up to all the time. There was a time that Jon told me (in reference to a period of misbehavior) that sometimes his brain wouldn't let him do the right thing. I thought and still do think that this statement said it all about kids with ADHD. How amazing that at such a young age he would figure out what was going on. He actually knew far more than the teachers he had had in the past.

## WILSON REMEDIATION IN THIRD GRADE

I think one of the most important classes for him that year was Wilson, a program that allows a dyslexic child to learn how to decode words and read. In the younger grades, he had fallen through cracks due to the fact that he was able to remember words that he had learned and thus appeared to be reading, even to the teachers, when actually he was just memorizing the words. Once language became more difficult at higher levels, one could see the hesitancy and lack of fluency.

I began to understand what Jon was going through. Those of us who can read take it so much for granted. There is some memorization and learning of sight words. But when we come to a word that we have never seen, we use tools that we have come to acquire naturally to sound it out. When children like Jon come to the same word, they become frustrated, and either quit, try to haphazardly sound it out, or substitute another word, which in many cases will change the meaning of the entire sentence. If he does unsuccessfully sound out the word, what comes out of his mouth is not a word that makes sense to him, most likely does not exist, and, on top of that, he has lost his fluency and therefore the meaning of the entire sentence. Children with dyslexia have trouble matching sounds to the letters. The characteristics of ADHD, impaired focus, inattentiveness, hyperactivity, and off task behavior only make the process of reading more confusing, frustrating, and difficult.

So third grade progressed without any major incidences. There were always times that he received yellow cards and warnings for his behavior. But overall, he would go off task and then be brought back by the behavior plan in place.

In addition to good behavior plans in school, attention also needed to be given to behavior at home, which at times was difficult. The behavior plan at school served to keep him on task and focused as much as possible. In addition, there are social issues for kids with ADHD as well. At least in the classroom, the behavior plan helped to keep Jon's impulsivity in check, which was often the root of evil for him. Blurting out, not taking turns, and physical outcomes like pushing and shoving and getting into others' personal spaces could adversely affect friendships with peers, and at least he would receive consequences for these in the school setting.

## CO-EXISTING CONDITIONS AT HOME

But at home, his relationships with his siblings were always at risk. First, he was the youngest of four kids, with a sister twenty-three years old, a brother eighteen years old, and a sister of sixteen. The tolerance level for his emotional immaturity was not there. Being teenagers, the others' maturity level was not always stable either! What could you expect?

Jonathan did and still does compete for the attention of his siblings. Unfortunately, he blurts out things and interrupts family conversations, and eventually he is screamed at for not listening. He does not promote patience in answering questions when he becomes obsessed with a certain topic and is relentless in his quest for details on that topic. No one knows any of those details and nor do they care about them!

It was and is not always easy to correct these problems. First, information is important. That is, the more information that family members have, the easier it is to tolerate and deal with Jon in an effective way. Siblings need to know that it is ok to get frustrated. Sometimes it is impossible to change the direction of a period of bad behavior. But it is ok to walk away from him after telling him that they are unable to deal with his anger, for instance, right now. He also needs to understand the impact of his behavior. ( which is sometimes the lack of communication with a sibling who is frustrated!) In addition, family counseling with a psychologist who has expertise in the area of ADHD is also recommended.

I would say that one of the serious co-existing conditions of ADHD is Jonathan's anxiety. This permeates everything he does. His level of anxiety is so heightened that it affects where he can be in his house. For example, during the day and night, he can not be on any level of the house where he would end up being alone. Even if someone goes up with him, they need to come down to his room with him so he can be comfortable with his surroundings.

Sleep is another source of fear and anxiety. When he was younger, he would start out sleeping in his room only to wake up at three a.m. and run down to our room. Over the past year or two, he has refused to sleep alone. He will only sleep with his teenage sister or with us, his parents. He seems to be afraid of noise, so he has figured out that in order to avoid any noise of unknown origin he needs to turn on his television.

Our learning consultant and advocate, Ms. Smith, referred us to a behavior psychologist who has a great deal of expertise in the area of ADHD. As was stated before, the combination of medication and psychological intervention works best in controlling behavior and also in dealing with co-existing conditions. In the spring of 2006, Jonathan and I went to see this psychologist. Both of us talked with him together initially and then separately. As we approached the end of the school year, life was becoming crazy and I stopped going to see him. I guess that was for a multitude of reasons. Maybe I had my doubts about how much this was helping him. Travel time was a half hour each way after school. Homework did not get done until after dinner, since we would return around that time. Delaying homework like that created a great deal of stress. The medication effect of increased focus was not there right after school anyway. But add that to a child exhausted from his day and you did not have focus or compliance. So the summer passed without any doctor's intervention.

## FOURTH GRADE: A TEACHER'S LACK OF KNOWLEDGE AND EMPATHY

The teachers, case manager, and my learning consultant met at the end of third grade to make sure that the correct IEP was in place so that Jonathan would receive the same support in fourth grade. He would again be in the resource room for math and reading. He would also be pulled from the regular class four times a week for a half hour for speech and language. Twice a week he would also receive continued support for decoding by learning Wilson fundamentals.

As was mentioned previously, Wilson fundamentals is a reading program that helps children learn to decode words and therefore read with more fluency. Many things are included in this process. They learn common sight words, trick words(words that do not follow rules of pronunciation), sounds that go with vowels both with and without consonants following them, and prefixes and suffixes. Jon would also have to show brackets for each part of a word. For instance, a two syllable word would be broken down into two parts, each with brackets. As you can imagine, this was quite tedious, but necessary to beable to understand the relationships of sounds to letters.

Once the fall returned and fourth grade began, Jon's level of anxiety and stress started to heighten. He actually asked when we were returning to Dr. P. I was stunned. And then I knew that we had found someone who he trusted and wanted to talk to on a weekly basis. He had sensed an understanding on Dr. P's part and did not want to let that part of his life go, despite the length of the drive, for which usually he had no tolerance. So I reassured him that we would return to Dr. P if that made him feel better.

Jon had a great desire to handle his fears. He had confidential talks with Dr. P, conversations that allowed Dr. P to understand just how anxious and fearful this child was at times. I would have the opportunity to sit with both of them to hear the content of the conversations. Also, I could interject anything that concerned me. We would come up with a plan to overcome obstacles that either interfered with his academics, social life, or home life.

It seemed to be an overwhelming schedule to which this child had to adjust. He not only had to be aware of the expectations of several teachers but had to also incorporate into his schedule added pullouts by the speech and Wilson teachers. A child already compromised with focus and anxiety issues was expected to stay on task for each teacher and to meet his or her expectations. In addition, another frustrating part was that the Wilson instruction took him out of science and social studies for periods of time that would certainly adversely affect his learning. Any hands-on learning offered in these subjects would at times be missed. But because Jonathan needed all of this support for now, I agreed.

Within the first two weeks of school, I received a call from Ms. D, Jon's special education teacher who ran the resource room and taught him math and reading. These classes contained five to six kids. Her concern was that Jon did not focus, did not follow directions, and had behavior issues that consisted of talking during the teaching of a lesson, yelling out, and just plain horsing around.

I was very concerned that a special education teacher would be calling me so early in the year. She seemed at a loss to control her classroom, with the result that Jonathan became a part of that loss of control. I remember thinking that the third-grade special education teacher, an expert at what she did, had never called me regarding any problems. I asked this fourth grade teacher if she had a behavior plan in place. I never really got the feeling that it was very specific, but she indicated that it existed.

Again, we as parents feel at a loss because we are not a part of the school setting. So to gather more information, I asked if we could start a communication journal that would allow me to understand what was going on in the class. Unfortunately, the journal rarely made it to the teacher because my child had the responsibility of getting it to her. And, of course, children with ADHD are disorganized and forgetful. Their short-term memory does not work efficiently. And remember, Jon must have felt out of control at times with the degree of pull-outs.

During this time, I received a call from this same teacher telling me that Jonathan had done poorly on a math test. She told me she would administer it again with more guidance and then average the two test grades together. I was horrified. From what Jon was telling me, there had been little guidance. It seemed that the test questions were all read in the beginning of class before the test, then everyone was asked if there were questions prior to taking the test. Apparently everyone was encouraged to ask questions throughout the test if needed.

What is wrong with this picture?? It certainly seemed to me (although I was told I was mistaken) that the teacher in this very small resource room, consisting of a handful of kids, had never taken the time to read Jon's IEP and understand him and his disability. A child with ADHD and a language-based learning disability with processing problems could not be expected to listen to all of the questions before taking a test, knowing what confusion he would encounter during the test. He also needed help reading each question prior to answering it. And to expect a child like Jon to ask for clarification of each question once the test began was ludicrous. He would have to have the self-esteem to ask the question, the courage to ask it again if confused, the comfort level with the teacher to continue to ask for help, and the academic ability to correctly read each question and understand the material being asked of him.

It would seem that if a child is placed in a resource room with a teacher certified in special education, he would not only be there to learn in his different way, but also to experience success. Instead there seemed to be no attempt to understand his disability or to help him find his way. Another episode of helplessness along our journey.

I put in a call to the case manager, asking her to please go to the classroom and find out what was going on regarding behavior and academics. It seemed that Jon was not successful in this setting, and his behavior was not contributing to his learning. It was agreed that Jon would take the test again, this time with each question read out loud. He was more successful this time. And, in addition to success, I am sure some learning occurred as well. Remember, IEP stands for individual educational plan. Goals and objectives are decided upon based on learning differences. Then, it is important to decide how they will be attained within the time frame decided upon. Many times, modification in the classroom is necessary for the success of attainment of goals. Reading questions out loud is just one of many modifications that can be put in place. Certainly, this would be an important modification where a child was dyslexic.

As we struggled to validate a behavior plan, Jon came home one day and told me that he had been put outside of the classroom to do a worksheet. Apparently he had been talking and the punishment was to remove him from the classroom. If he had a question, he could come into the class and ask. Once banished from the classroom, I am sure that Jonathan did not have the comfort level to walk back in and ask anything. In addition, if he had high levels of confusion, as I am sure that he intermittently did, he may not have known what to ask.

I called Ms. D and inquired as to the circumstances behind this horrendous decision to ban my son from the class. My feeling was that this was a teacher who could not handle my son; a certified special education teacher who, when she could not handle him or how he was apparently disrupting the class, decided to throw him out. She had previously said to me that he was unfocused and could not follow multi-step directions. He would simply shut down, allowing his frustration to prevent any success.

At one point she said that students must work very hard to focus. That statement, without a doubt, showed me that this teacher had no clue as to the dynamics of ADHD. She was saying that if Jon really wanted to focus, he could. One of the many fallacies of ADHD is that these children can control their behavior, both in terms of impulsivity and level of focus. As per Dr. Barkley, it is not the lack of knowledge of what should be done; it is the lack of ability to act on that knowledge. That is, if he could focus without distraction, he would, since he knew that this was what he should do in order to learn. Since ADHD is a medical diagnosis, it would be just as ludicrous to say and believe that it is possible for someone with hypertension to control his blood pressure. And it would demonstrate a severe lack of understanding of the pathophysiology of the illness.

A multitude of emotions flooded within me. Anger and helplessness were at the top of the list.

On each individual question when taking a test, my question to the teacher would be: "And how do you know that my son was not doing his best?? How do you know that it even was a focus problem?" Maybe, given the fact that he has a significant learning disability, it was a combination of focus and of actually processing the meaning of the question. Without understanding the meaning of the question, it seems rather difficult to be able to ask a question. I also believe that, in addition to all of that, there was a degree of anxiety that hampered Jon's ability to be successful. Certainly he knew that the work was difficult and the teacher not supportive. He had to be asking himself, "Why can't I do this? Why is this teacher not accepting me?"

It became clear that this teacher's behavior plan did not exist as she had said. I was devastated and yet determined to make changes for my son. She did not see what she needed to see. I did not believe that even this teacher could grasp the difficulties that surrounded Jon. He had an invisible diagnosis that she, like many, I am convinced, forget about. She did not see it, so therefore it did not exist to impede him. But with his lack of compliance in her classroom came her frustration. Her negative responses to his lack of focus and disruption only accentuated his behavior. With her negative consequences came his anger…anger because of his embarrassment and lower self-esteem, because no matter how many times she said he should ask questions, he knew that he could not because he did not know what to ask, and so he continued acting out (talking and fooling around) in order to avoid those things that he knew he could not do.

## THE FORMULATION OF A BEHAVIOR PLAN IN SCHOOL

I would change things. I couldn't successfully teach Ms. D about ADHD, but I could make sure that a behavior plan was in place in the classroom. Perhaps, as the behavior plan became successful as seen by Jon becoming more productive and less disruptive, the teacher would begin to understand.

An IEP meeting was scheduled for the middle of October 2006. It had been previously scheduled because, by law, his eligibility for special education services had to be reviewed every three years. So now we would certainly have more to talk about.

As mentioned previously, I had started taking Jonathan again to the psychologist, Dr. P. I decided that I needed him to be involved with the behavior plan in school. I had Ms. D e-mail him and talk about behaviors that concerned her. She told him pretty much the same thing regarding behaviors that were disruptive to learning. Before setting up a plan, Dr. P suggested raising his Concerta by five mg. So, before the medication dose was changed, behavior rating scales were handed out to all of the teachers who came in contact with Jon. It seemed that there definitely were some focus concerns, but these were mainly showing up in the resource room. Without telling the teachers, his dose was raised by five mg followed by the necessity of filling out more behavior rating scales by his teachers in order to determine whether this dose made the difference.

Jonathan continued to have trouble in Ms. D's class with focus and behavior. Interestingly, with the increase in medication, his behavior really did not change much in the resource room environment. Research states that behavior is best managed by medication and behavioral psychology. Behavioral psychology could include both school and home behavior plans and intervention from a therapist. Here was a real life example of that. Medication alone was not making a difference in Jon's academic life. Responses to Jonathan's disruptive behavior were punitive in nature. Not only were these responses damaging to the teacher-student relationship, but they simply were not working. The relationship was not positive between the teacher and Jon. So began another journey within my journey.

During the IEP of October, this behavior problem was discussed. It was decided that the school psychologist would speak to Dr. P about an appropriate behavior plan that would be conducive to learning for Jon. Dr. Smith, my learning consultant, was present and made a comment about why the behavior plan from last year did not follow Jon into this year. His special education teacher, Ms. D, began to cry. I then realized to my horror that this teacher thought everything was about her. Was she that narcissistic that the needs of Jon were secondary to hers??

I wondered what motivated a person such as her to place herself in a profession that demanded the ability to assess and remediate a child's learning issues; a selfless task, no doubt. I knew then that I needed to stay focused on Jon's needs throughout the year. If the teacher admitted failure on Jon's part in any way, would she see this as a personal assault on herself and her abilities and therefore not deal with it? I didn't know...Pure speculation on my part, I understand, but nevertheless, speculation that would prompt me to be vigilant.

There was a halt to negative and punitive responses for Jon until a positive behavior plan was put into place. Unfortunately, the development of this plan was laborious. Conversations between the school psychologist and Dr. P were primarily via e-mail. This could and did lead to some misunderstanding. The school psychologist eventually put the plan in place, but it was not the plan that Dr. P had advocated. I believe that this young professional wanted to make a name for herself and did not want to fully follow this older and more experienced psychologist. I guess maybe ego and turf were at the forefront of the problem. But to me, Jon's needs were priority. If I had a relationship with a professional who possessed a tremendous amount of experience in this area of behavior modification, I intended to use his expertise. This young school psychologist needed to look at him as a gift...a beautiful learning experience with which she could incorporate techniques and knowledge for the good of children with ADHD to come down her path.

Why not embrace this knowledge?

I suggested that instead of using e-mails, which only by their nature encouraged misunderstandings, both psychologists needed to meet and discuss the issues. Precious time was passing. Jonathan needed immediate intervention in that resource room. For him, it was a war zone: his anger was heightened, his academics were not improving, and his self-esteem was declining.

So Dr. P agreed to come to the school district and speak directly to the special education teacher, the case manager, and the school psychologist. It was suggested that I not attend. As a result of this meeting, a positive behavior plan was put in place. Prior to this plan, the behavior plan was very publicly negative. Marking on the board when he received a point for inappropriate behavior created embarrassment and did not work to reinforce the positive behavior. In addition, it made Jon feel that he was disliked and bad.

# DISCIPLINE AND THE POINT SYSTEM

The new plan decided on target behaviors that would be assessed as being acceptable or not. Although the school psychologist wanted to set the targeted behaviors as remaining seated, remaining quiet, and following directions, Dr. P disagreed, believing that they were too ambiguous. After all, there were times within the day where it was permissible to walk around and talk. He suggested a color wheel as a visual stimulus. Red on the wheel would correspond to the need to be seated and work on a given assignment. Yellow could mean that it would be permissible to walk around quietly. Green could mean snack time, or time during which it was permissible to talk and play.

Each work period would start out with a given number of points. Dr. P said that this system worked much better with these kids when they started out with a set number of points and then worked not to lose them. If a point was lost due to inappropriate behavior, it did not have to be a personal event or a confrontation. Simply, the child lost a point on a chart. At the time of the loss, he was aware of it, but it was not discussed with him or the class. Also it was important for the teacher to make positive comments during the day when Jon was complying with the rules. It has been shown that reinforcing positive behavior with positive comments and rewards is much more effective than overly responding to negative behavior. That negative behavior directs attention to him.

To Jon, despite the fact it is negative attention, it is still attention that he has achieved. The stimulus of negative attention only reinforces future negative behavior. By reinforcing the positive behavior, it is thought that more positive behavior will occur, with less time for negative behavior. Incorporated into the behavior plan would be rewards in school for acceptable behavior. It was determined that rewards could be such privileges as being a class monitor or erasing the board. Points achieved throughout the week would come home so that we could also reinforce his successes.

## A SUDDEN ALTERATION IN THE BEHAVIOR PLAN

Things in the classroom seemed to get better regarding Jon's behavior once the plan was put in place at the end of October. The holidays came and went and it was now time to start school again in January. But behavior plans that were supposed to come home suddenly were no longer. Jonathan seemed sullen and quiet when he came home from school, yet he would not really express any problems. When I finally asked for the behavior plans to be sent home with Jon, I realized that they did not seem to be what we had discussed. No points seemed to be earned, only stars, which was not the point system that had been advocated by Dr. P. In addition, it was not clear what behaviors were being targeted. They were only numbered.

One day, the behavior plan showed that there were losses in a given area that lead to no star for some unnamed activity. When asked, Jon said that the activity was snack time. There was not supposed to be any expectations for that activity since it was free time, I thought. But something had happened and he told me that he had lost snack time and was required to do a worksheet!

I was concerned about his academics and did not know what battles I should fight. I let this go for a couple of weeks until another incident occurred that I could no longer ignore. In addition, things that Jon was telling me were giving me heightened concern. Each week Jon had to do a spelling packet that now included the writing of sentences, which was a challenge given his dyslexia. I was a huge support to him because of his struggles. He would come up with an idea for a sentence and when it was not really an example of a fourth-grade sentence, I would add to it. I thought that by modeling, I could eventually teach him.

## UNREALISTIC EXPECTATIONS

One day, I asked him to write his sentences without my support because I could not be there. After a major meltdown, he proceeded to write eight sentences using his eight spelling words. When I saw them later, I knew that the sentences were not acceptable for his age. Although good ideas, there was no punctuation, it was sloppy, and, in most cases, too brief. But I decided to let him send it in so the teacher could see what happened when there was no support.

What happened next was unexpected. She decided to have Jon re-do four sentences. This was without help from her and without direction. When he returned to school the next day without the assignment (since because of his schedule and lack of focus and fatigue after a long day, he simply could not fit in any more homework) she sent back a missing homework paper that now said that he would lose points for the entire packet. He seemed stressed and upset. He told me that she told him that if it did not come back the next day, he would lose recess.

Now, Jon was in a resource room with four kids for reading. During that day, the teacher asked him if he needed help on the sentences, since he did not return them for homework. Now, my husband and I wondered, how does a certified special education teacher who teaches four kids in a resource room ask a special needs child with dyslexia and ADHD if he NEEDS HELP? Could anyone help us with that???? It seemed to us that she should have recognized the need for support and direction on the day the sentences were originally handed in for homework.

On this same day, we had visited Dr. P. and I told him about this frustrating bit of information because it did relate to the behavior plan: negative consequence (no recess) for not redoing homework. First of all, kids with ADHD should never have recess pulled from them because they focus better as a result of having it. Secondly, as Dr. P pointed out, Jon was being punished for not controlling something that was not in his power to control (writing). He suggested that Jon and I attach words to his spelling words in order for him to come up with a good sentence. To avoid the added stress of him trying to remember the sentence he thought of and then transferring it to paper, he would try to think of a good sentence using the cues for each spelling word and I would type each sentence as he spoke. And that's what we did to accomplish this task. Again, disorganization and a lack of short-term memory made this task quite a challenge for Jon.

## FIGHTING BACK

I sent an e-mail to the teacher, indicating my frustration at her lack of support for Jonathan. Even his regular education teacher understood him better. She knew that to allow for focus and frustration levels, his work many times had to be modified. Modification does not translate into re-doing homework without support from a teacher. Apparently I had lent too much support. This teacher was unable to realize that homework many times was a result of a lot of support from me. But by this time, the end of February, you would expect that from comparing his work in class, she would be very aware of his strengths and limitations.

When I asked for support, I got nothing but an argumentative e-mail sent to the principal. She said that I agreed in an IEP meeting that Jon was not exempt from homework. She said that his homework was sloppy and unreadable and that she had simply asked for him to redo half of the sentences. She denied the threat of loss of recess. The principal, without commenting to me, sent me this reply, which really was not meant for me. I responded to him, saying that everything I had previously said was the truth. I never advocated exempting Jon from homework. I only expected him to be taught.

I guess I continued to be stunned by this teacher's response to a distraught parent. I did my best to not show anger, just concern and frustration. She probably took everything I said personally. My expectation of a professional teacher, one who was also certified to teach special education, was apparently too high. She could have handled this in a far more effective way by helping my son with his writing skills. Instead, she found it necessary to defend herself and her actions to her supervisor, her principal.

It is clear to me why there are so many kids who do fall through the cracks in education; special needs kids whose disability is invisible. They are pushed through the system and graduate from high school without the ability to read. And why does this happen even today in this twenty-first century? Is it a lack of knowledge as to what kids who learn differently require? Is it apathy on the part of those who are supposed to be supervising teachers who are new to their field? Are people too busy to adequately assess those who need it? Is the system prioritizing children who can learn with ease within the current system? Is it also a financial burden to do the job right?

I believe that all of the above contain a matter of truth. And that is why it is imperative that we as parents stay vigilant and must advocate for our children. We must never feel inadequate in the field of education. Those of us who are not teachers know what our limitations are, but we know in our hearts when our children are suffering. We do have an obligation and a right to be there for them and to fight for what is their right to have: an education, a right to learn in the way that they know how, and, while that is happening, a self-esteem that is healthy and strong.

Because of all of the above, my fourth-grade son ended up with a special education teacher who was tenured and apparently untouchable, without an incredible amount of documentation regarding her apparent lack of skills and inability to deal with the impulsive, hyperactive, and lack of focus aspects that comprise the behavior of my son and others with ADHD. Because of his language-based learning deficits, he has trouble processing verbal directions. Can you imagine a special education teacher, after being asked a question about an activity, telling a child that it was already explained and that he should know better now that he is in fourth grade? Can you imagine what this does to a child's self-esteem? A child just reaching an age that allows him to wonder why he can't sit still, why he can't learn the way others do...leading him to not believe in himself, to believe that his peers do not believe in him and that he is not worthy of their friendship. In a child's mind, a teacher is supposed to teach and believe in him. If he does not think that she does, he must truly be a lost cause.

In March, we had requested testing to better advocate a change from resource room to regular classroom. I thought that if I could minimize the amount of time this special education teacher, Ms. D, impacted his life, it could only be good. Unfortunately, a director of special education, Mr. Z, as well as the principal, were not supportive of this change. Because the testing showed that Jon was borderline in his ability to do fourth grade math, he was transferred into Ms. G's regular education math class. Now he would be in a class of 22, requiring him to focus, not become distracted, and move at the pace of the class. He would also have an aid to help him, although she would be helping others in the class as well. It was not optimal for Jon. But again, I was concerned about how his self-esteem was being affected by Ms. D and was therefore willing to make the move since he showed an ability to perform math on grade level. We hoped that his borderline ability would allow adequate performance despite the increase in the number of children in the general education class and with it, an increase in distraction for Jon.

## POSITIVE MOVE TO AVOID CONTINUED NEGATIVITY

Ms. G was the kind of teacher you seldom meet. At least in my years of raising children, she was a rarity. In a class of twenty-two, she was able to assess abilities and knew what children needed. In addition, she knew how to encourage, support, and therefore allow a child to know that if he worked hard enough, he just may get it!! My son needed a great deal of support in this classroom. We kept in touch with each other as to how Jon was making it through this class. She had a true admiration for this child who desperately wanted to be part of the big group, who wanted to succeed, who wanted his teacher to be proud of him. Positive reinforcement was effective while negative responses only reinforced oppositional and negative behavior in Jon. This was so dramatically shown in his academic settings. Negative behavior and poor academic performance occurred in the resource room with a teacher who had no tolerance or understanding of ADHD. Positive behavior and success in academics could be seen in the general education classroom where the teacher was positive and understanding. I will always remember this teacher who worked so hard to promote a very sagging self-esteem in my son. Jon will remember her, too!

I went in for a parent-teacher conference. Before we sat down to look at paperwork, Ms. G called me over to the computer. She showed me what she was doing with the class that day. Projected onto a screen was a problem that consisted of several clues as to the number she was looking for, clues like "larger than twenty-five," "divisible by two," "even number," etc. She said that the entire class struggled with this yet Jon kept raising his hand with the correct answer!! This child, one with profound language-based learning disabilities, ADHD, and anxieties, the child in this room on a shoe string who used every bit of energy to focus in class for the grueling forty minutes, was the winner!!!

This teacher was stunned and proud. You know I was delighted and proud, but not really surprised. I knew that kids like Jon were simply wired differently. (Even his kindergarten teacher, before he was officially diagnosed, used that phrase!) Here was a beautiful example of a learning disabled child with ADHD who showed his average-to-above-average intelligence. On required tests and papers he many times faltered and always needed one-on-one support, but the manner in which these problems were presented allowed him to shine. He was able to pull information from all of the clues thrown out and come up with the answer. Can you just imagine how thrilled he was when he was the first to figure out the problems?!

Ironically, he never told me. But again, I guess this is a product of ADHD. Despite it being a wonderful moment, he never really focused on it long enough to brag about himself! And certainly, lack of short-term memory affected his ability to retrieve something that happened during the school day.

So, despite Ms. G's supportive teaching style that was contributing to Jon's success in the general education classroom, I had a special education teacher who not only was not teaching and supporting Jon, she was no longer communicating to me. She decided that I was off base and incorrect in my statements and took everything personally. Again, it was all about her, not the education of my son.

What a stark difference between the regular classroom where Jon learned math and this resource room where special needs children sought understanding, support, and small class instruction with acceptance.

## GOALS AND OBJECTIVES NOT BEING MET IN THE RESOURCE ROOM: A FIGHT

I called my learning consultant, Dr. Smith, after forwarding her the e-mails that had been sent. She did show some anger to me. She felt that I did not understand that this teacher had tenure and that there was no way I was going to change that. She believed that my interventions were escalating problems and worsening the situation, without hope of a positive outcome.

Maybe she was right, but being a mom, sometimes it is tough to allow things to go on that will not help my son achieve success. I did not understand why I was alone in the area of teaching my child. Good grades are delightful to put on a paper. To some teachers, I guess, it means that they are successful in teaching…and it means that there are no glaring problems. When I sent Jon's sentences in without supporting them like I had done in the past, Ms. D was horrified. By demanding them to be done over, was she insinuating that he had control over his disability? Did she really think that all of the sentences done in the past were completely done by him without support? He was in a resource room with a special education teacher because he learned differently. Multi-sensory techniques to learn required material as well as remediation of his dyslexia and reinforcement were all things to be provided in the resource room that were not in the regular education classes.

Despite the fact that we together did those sentences over, Jon remained very stressed. He could not verbalize it, but maybe he was just in a setting where he couldn't predict unpredictable and impossible demands placed on him.

Two days later, Dr. Smith called me. She had been speaking to another case manager in another elementary school in town. She told her about what had transpired with the resource room teacher. She told her who it was. Apparently Dr. Smith got the impression that there had been problems regarding this teacher in the past. This other case manager strongly encouraged her to have me write a letter to the director of special education, stating my concerns that included the fact that goals and objectives in my son's IEP were not being met. This teacher was below par for the district and a meeting was necessary to determine alternatives either within the district or outside the district.

I did write the letter over the weekend. A meeting was set up within a week to discuss the problems. In addition, the case manager for Jon was to have some informal test results in place. They would be informal, like the testing which was done last year, so that we would be comparing apples to apples. Attendees at the meeting would be my learning consultant, Dr. Smith, the case manager, Ms. B, the principal, Mr. L, my husband and me, and Mr. Z.

Prior to the meeting, Mr. Z had called Dr. Smith, my learning consultant. Apparently, one of the offers on the table was to send Jon to another elementary school within the district where the resource room teacher was strong and the principal had a doctorate in special education. My husband was very disturbed by this alternative. It seemed to us that changing Jon's environment in the middle of the year would create a high level of anxiety in a kid who already was anxious. The camaraderie he had with neighborhood kids would dwindle. He no longer would be at the same bus stop, on the same bus, or in the same school.

The meeting took place on a Thursday morning. Another part of advocating for your child that is very difficult when you are not a teacher is not allowing personnel to intimidate you. They know the law, they presumably know education, and they are pretty sure that you know neither! The case manager had the results of the testing she had done. The test results as presented to me were confusing. I decided to verbalize what I considered to be the bottom line. In the area of third grade, scores were stated in the area of "frustration." In the area of second grade, scores were listed as "instructional." I directed my question to the case manager when I asked if what I was interpreting was correct. That is, Jonathan was academically on a second-grade level. She said that I was correct in that assessment. (Remember, he was now in fourth grade.) Apparently, he was not at the level of third grade material since it was too frustrating to him as seen by test scores. That is at least how I interpreted this segment of the meeting. No one really appeared to want to further explain.

A couple of minutes later, Mr. Z started talking about percentages and tried to indicate that it looked as though Jon was doing better. Because I had just clarified what I knew to be true, I looked at him and said," as was confirmed by the case manager, Jonathan is over two years behind in the area of language. Actually, he was two years behind by the last testing, so actually he was now farther behind than before. Certainly no strides have occurred during fourth grade, thereby reinforcing the original accusation of goals and objectives not being obtained." He looked at me and surprisingly actually stopped talking!! It appeared to me at that instant that I had just lived another moment in this journey where a teacher tried to comfort me falsely! I was outraged, but at the same time, proud of myself for having confirmed the facts before he could start his dance routine.

So began the rest of the mostly uncomfortable meeting. The principal, Mr. L, was angry because, as I had indicated before, I had placed Jon in the regular education class for math because the resource room was such a negative experience for him. His testing had allowed it, although his ADHD was certainly getting in the way. I was aware of this, but to me it had been a better choice. He said that Jon was the lowest functioning student in the resource room (indicating that he certainly had no business being in the regular classroom). He then said that it was wrong and impossible to force a curriculum on a child; presumably that is how he saw it. To me, he was indicating that we were forcing difficult information on a child incapable of producing.

But I had another point. I said to him, "I agree, Mr. L, a teacher should not force a curriculum on a child who is unable to do the work. This premise should also be applied to the resource room. A child who is having difficulty should not be expected to perform in the same way as the next child. The special education teacher in that resource room should be able to modify her special education curriculum according to the needs of her students. This was clearly not being done for my son and is the main reason for this meeting." In effect, I used their words and terminology to express my points!

After some silence, Mr. Z nodded his head and stated quite emphatically that he would go into the resource room, meet Jon, and write with him. He would need two weeks to evaluate and come back to us with a proposal. He asked me if that would be ok with me. Although I knew that time was needed, my initial response was no, it really was not ok. Two weeks was a lifetime for Jon and me to wait for a solution to the problem. After all, it was now coming to the end of February and there was no time to waste.

It just felt like the kind of statement that was pushing me away, as I had often felt throughout my journey: a pat on the head, it's ok, I need to calm down, he is doing fine, he is progressing, etc. All of those statements I had heard throughout my journey. Now in fourth grade, with my child over two years behind, I could no longer stand being told anything that would make me wait. But unfortunately, I had no choice once again. But this time maybe I was taken a little more seriously. I would have to wait the two weeks to see how we were to move our son forward.

In addition, during this meeting, Jon's psychologist was available via speaker phone. He talked about kids with ADHD in general. Some of the characteristics fall throughout the spectrum of children's personalities. But more kids with ADHD are laden with characteristics that would create many problems when changing an academic environment abruptly, which was what was being proposed. Jon's anxieties and his need for familiarity and structure would certainly hinder this advocated change offered by professionals who really ought to know better! Jon, like many kids with ADHD, have anxieties about a lot of things. And as they get older, they begin to realize that they are different from other kids. Their lack of focus can hinder their learning, and, as in Jon's case, many are struggling with learning disabilities as they try to learn in a very rigid environment. It was clear that Dr. P was not a proponent for sending Jon to another school in district as previously proposed. And we then were not either.

My husband, present at one of his first meetings that concerned the education of his son, believed that it was important to reinforce the fact that there was an apparent lack of supervision. After all, here was a teacher who, at twenty-eight years old, was tenured. So I guess in the minds of the union and all those who were tenured themselves, they were untouchable without a lot of documentation. Documentation and time were not on our side. As I have said before, where are the supervisors who oversee what is being done in the classroom? After all, every work setting has supervisory personnel.

To our minds, the school, even before we got there, had failed our son.

Remember, I had previously sent Jon's tests to the public school's child study team when he was in the catholic school, asking for their opinion. At the time, I was told that Jon would not receive any more support in public school than he was currently receiving. He was doing fine in Catholic school. In other words, he would be fine right where he was.

So now I faced a child study team in the public school setting where my son was still not receiving appropriate intervention. Certainly, the comment about receiving enough support in Catholic school was proven to be completely false. The public school system did not even have the researched programs for remediation of a language based learning disability in place nor did they have staff who could administer it. In addition, it seemed to me that there was really no one who understood ADHD.

I did not bring up the past in this meeting in an effort to maintain civility and not prompt negativity and to avoid damaging the ability to get Jon what he needed. But ironically, as Mr. Z was trying to portray himself as someone who had dealt with me in the past (and apparently thought he was extremely helpful), his condescending reassurances made me want to visit those issues from two years ago. You can imagine how angry it made me.

My learning consultant, who was aware of this, smiled and told him that he probably did not want to go there. She was prompted to say this after he commented on how he has always been there for me! I said that I needed to move on, since I had promised to be civil. His expression was priceless. It was a combination of confusion and embarrassment. He later came to me after the meeting to shake my hand and apologize for anything that may have happened in the past to cause me frustration and stress. I pulled my hand away and just stared. I could not honestly say that it was ok…because it was not.

I bring up this incident again because it represents the essence of this book. Advocating for your child is absolutely imperative. Even when you doubt yourself, always question everything. Never feel inferior when you are asking questions of those in the educational forum. People generally expect those educated in other areas to be the experts who can answer everything and will always make the right decisions. But unfortunately, that is just not the case. Whether it is ignorance, money, apathy, or lack of time, people in the educational system may not be totally on your side. It is not always easy to figure out who it is that we can trust and in whom we can believe. So the number one person who you can trust is yourself…start there.

So we waited the long two weeks so that Mr. Z could visit Jon's classroom and complete his evaluation of academics and behavior. It seemed like such a long time to wait. I wanted results and change…and I also was worried that some of this would have some impact on how Jon would be treated. I have been told by many educational experts that teachers do not take out their anger on their students. In other words, if the teacher does not like you the parent, or not like your behavior on the child's behalf, this does not alter her teaching style and behavior toward the child. I certainly hope this is true…But I am sure that is not always the case.

## AN ATTEMPT TO IMPROVE THE MEETING OF IEP GOALS

So another meeting convened with Mr. Z, the case manager, my learning consultant, and me. Mr. Z, of course, had glowing comments of praise for my son, including things like wanting to please and working hard. This feedback came from visiting the resource room teacher, Ms. D. However, I always feel as though comments like that are somewhat demeaning to the intelligence of the parent. They serve to mask the severity of the issue...We as parents of special needs children do not need or want "feel good" statements. If we are true advocates for our children, we already know what makes up their personalities. We know their strengths and weaknesses. We encourage the strengths and gifts that they possess in order to help them compensate for their difficulties and thereby raise their self-esteem and help them succeed in this often very difficult world.

Mr. Z also made a comment about how Jon needed to move. He at times felt it necessary to sit on the heating vents in the classroom and look out of the window. Now, of course, this again did not surprise me, knowing him. But he followed that comment with how understanding his teacher was to his needs to move. From previous complaints throughout the year, I knew this was a definite falsehood. But I think his statement was twofold...By that statement, he defended his teacher by making sure that I knew that she understood the nature of ADHD. In addition, it was important to give me a sense of comfort for what was to follow next in this conversation.

Mr. Z suggested starting a reading program called SRA. I was told that SRA was a program that would remediate dyslexia. It would be done in the resource room for Jon and another child whose reading level was similar. It would necessitate an aide being present during the thirty to forty minutes of program administration to manage the other three kids in the room. In order to administer this, a teacher needed to be certified. His current resource room teacher, Ms. D, of course, was certified.

Our initial goal was to fight for a change for Jon. This would mean changing resource room teachers in addition to content. Now here it was the beginning of March. No school would start trying to hire someone new now...and probably would not succeed in finding someone qualified anyway. It appeared that the reality of the situation was that we would have Ms. D for the rest of the year. But at least we had accomplished a couple of things. First, we brought our issues to the people who needed to hear them in order to affect change. We initiated a new reading program that would hopefully move Jon forward in his level of reading. It seemed very objective; a program that could easily be followed and monitored without the teacher being able to make changes or refuse to follow it. This teacher happened to be certified in the administration of this program. In addition, the teaching of the program would be done in a group of two children; a number that would certainly facilitate learning for Jon, increasing his ability to focus as well as increasing the duration of focus and on task behavior.

## THE JOURNEY SHOWING THE NEED TO ALWAYS ADVOCATE AS A PARENT

So the question remained in my head....I turned to my learning consultant and asked her why we were going through all of this stress and controversy. It was well documented that Jon was significantly behind in reading. He was placed in a resource room with five kids with a certified special education teacher. This teacher was certified in the program of SRA. SRA is a comprehensive reading program that helps children with decoding and comprehension. It is meant for grades 4-12 and for children who are one or more grade levels below grade placement. It focuses on word attack skills and reading in a group. It insures individual mastery as well. It does have a piece of comprehension that includes instruction in thinking strategies. It is structured and scripted and does not allow for a teacher's interpretation on how to administer it. In this case, that would be a positive characteristic of this program. Why had all of this time been wasted? Why, after a parent initiated meeting, was this program just beginning in March?

There were no answers. MY ANSWER: Once again, evidence shows that it is imperative that parents advocate for their special needs children; in this case, their ADHD children. Never assume that because something is the right thing to do, that it will be done. Sometimes, I think it is easier, cheaper, and less stressful to do what's best for the majority, the group. Even in a small setting, like a resource room with five children, teaching to the level of learning that is most prevalent works for the school system. The child that can't keep up with the rest of the class is left behind. But it is so subtle and less dramatic than you would think. He may not understand and may feel uncomfortable about letting anyone know because he sees that everyone else seems to be doing fine.

I have seen this situation countless times concerning Jon. I have many times asked him why he does not ask a question if he does not understand. My feeling, at least in this case, is that he feels the expectation is that he does understand. If he admits anything other than that, he will feel stupid. These feelings do not just come from him. They have been suggested and substantiated by comments made by the teacher. "Try to do it yourself, you should be able to do that." He hears these comments throughout the year, and I truly believe that much of the teacher's reaction is based on her lack of understanding of ADHD and all of the co-existing conditions. After all, this is the disability that is truly invisible. Without a clear understanding of this disability and because people cannot see it, the effects of it, like impulsivity and lack of focus, are believed to be controlled by the child. Nothing could be farther from the truth.

## INITIATION OF SRA

So from March to the end of fourth grade, Jonathan received this new reading program SRA during resource room for forty minutes a day. He didn't seem too happy with it at times. But I think it was just the result of the negativity in the resource room that had forever altered his relationship with that teacher. Her persistent lack of understanding of ADHD and of him created in him a lack of trust and a lowered self-esteem. The damage was done. But at least the program was set up and the objectivity and guidelines were set. This structure would be positive for Jon. At least he would know what would be expected of him. That in itself was very important. Kids with ADHD thrive much better in a structured environment. Hopefully that would help him to overcome any judgmental attitudes on the part of the teacher.

## PLANNING FOR 5ᵀᴴ GRADE

In early June we had another IEP meeting to plan for fifth grade. I had heard that the resource room teacher for fifth grade was very experienced and positive. Because Jon had such a difficult time being mainstreamed during part of fourth grade for math, it was suggested that he be placed back in the resource room for both math and reading. I agreed because I knew that it was true that the environment was very stressful for him. He had only been placed there because of the negativity in the resource room. In addition, he had been on a pass/fail grade system in social studies and science because of the degree of pull-outs. During chunks of time during both subjects, he had been pulled for additional reading help, Wilson training. It was suggested that this continue, but to substitute Wilson with the previous SRA reading program.

Late in June, I thought more about all of the above. Again, I think we as parents have to worry about the whole child. By that I mean that, along with the ability to be academically successful, the necessity of having an intact self-esteem is vital. If you are able to achieve, but don't believe that you really can, what is the outcome? The answer lies in motivation. If you don't believe in yourself, you will not be motivated to try. The end result is failure, despite your real ability.

I started to focus on that. Were the benefits outweighing the risks with all of these pull-outs? I began to realize that Jon was the most pulled out child in that school. Even a child without ADHD would have trouble staying focused on all of the transitions in his day. In addition, he was with the mainstream class less than he was with his friends in resource room. I started to feel that he really did not have much of a connection with his class because he was really always on the move. And as experts have stated, a feeling of connectivity is imperative for a healthy self-esteem.

The other part of this was the lack of accountability in social studies and science. There was a lack of communication between parent and teacher because he was seen as the kid who was never there. Although he was to take tests as a learning tool, he still saw all of the red marks on his paper, indicating a poor job. Of course, many times I did not know about a test. He, of course, was not always willing to tell me. The bar was lowered in these classes...and as a result, so was his motivation.

I e-mailed the case manager in early July asking for changes in Jon's IEP. I was told that no changes would take place until the beginning of the school year when a meeting would take place with all personnel present. I was frustrated because I did not want this meeting to take place in October. I needed it to be in place for the beginning of the year for Jon's sake. Unfortunately, I had not made these decisions at the previous meeting. I do feel responsible for this. But sometimes things take a while to figure out.

In late August, I again tried to communicate with the case manager, the principal and my learning consultant. I had trouble connecting with anyone initially, except the learning consultant's office.

Eventually, Mr. Z called me and reassured me that Jon could start the year mainstreamed in social studies and science without pull-outs for SRA. Now he was telling me that a meeting would be necessary to put this in place. A meeting was to be set up once school started. I would not let him off the phone until he committed to me that a meeting would be set up now rather than delay that decision for later consideration. I did not want this meeting to get pushed far out into the future. He agreed. I asked him who I would hear from regarding the date and time of the meeting. He said he would call me with that information, and he did.

So on the second day of school, an IEP meeting took place. My concerns were discussed regarding Jon's level of motivation and self-esteem. Everyone seemed to be in agreement, but all of them were guarded regarding his abilities in those classes.  It was known that the science teacher was extremely demanding, testing the kids on very hard material.

The social studies teacher, also Jon's homeroom teacher, was present at the meeting and was very affable. He was young and new at teaching, but I sensed a genuine feeling of caring. He seemed to really like teaching and did not seem to just prioritize the kids who did well. He was in agreement that he has and would in the future work with the resource room teacher regarding reasonable expectations for Jon. The resource room teacher would make sure that he would take modified tests so that expectations would be reasonable and he would then feel successful. This would also go for the science tests.

My other concern was negating any speech and language services that were to take place during any of his classes. I told the group of professionals, the speech teacher, the social studies teacher, the case manager, my learning consultant, the resource room teacher, and the very young and new principal, that I would be willing to take Jonathan to a private speech therapist to avoid continued pull-outs. The speech teacher still wanted to provide her services because she had a good relationship with Jon and wanted to continue to help him.

So the question was determining when she would work with Jon. I said that it would be a great idea if this therapy took place during art class. Jon hated art, probably for a myriad of reasons, including a teacher with expectations that he could not fulfill. Not all of us are artists...or want to be.

The new principal spoke up as he continued to write his notes and declared that he would not allow any pull-outs during the specials since this was a time that children could express themselves and thereby boost self-esteem. To me, that was an outrageous statement. Children's self-esteem is based on individual desires, gifts, and abilities...not based on what someone else says will make them feel good, especially kids with ADHD. Not being around a teacher with unreasonable expectations could certainly boost self-esteem in a child. And secondly, I found it amazing that he would not think it just as important not to miss important class time...time that translated into knowledge and understanding of material so that there was a capability to score well on exams and thereby feel good about oneself!!

The only reason that I did not argue with him at the time was that the social studies teacher came up with a period of time that would allow Jon to go to speech and not miss class; a time where he could go over expectations for language, a subject for which Jon typically went to resource room. So this was agreed upon.

Being a young and very inexperienced principal, I got the sense that Mr. L had never been a part of an IEP meeting. He took notes furiously. Maybe that's why he felt so compelled to contribute to the meeting when he announced his disdain for pulling students during specials. At least he could say something. At one point, he looked up from his notes and asked me a question. We had been talking about medication and about my frustration with several areas about medicating: feeling comfortable giving it, picking the right one for your child, and assuring that the dosage is correct. He asked me why I did not give the meds on the weekend.

Now, I guess I could have given him the benefit of the doubt and said that he was in a learning mode and was gathering information. But somehow it didn't feel like that. Maybe I was biased because of previous negative experiences with teaching professionals, I don't know. But it seems that if someone were gathering information about these stimulants, he might ask how they worked in a child with ADHD. Now if he already knew that, then perhaps that question was putting me on the defensive, which is how I felt.

So I answered him, "Mr. L, if you are asking me if there needs to be a blood level for efficacy, the answer is no…Stimulants work right away, and then they are out of the system. So many times parents decide to give their kids a break from the meds on weekends and holidays, especially if they somewhat hamper appetite. Sometimes the older child will verbalize the need to just be themselves without medication intervention."

So the IEP was changed to allow for achieving grades in social studies and science. I had asked Jon prior to this meeting if that would make him happy. He said yes, that he would love not getting pulled out of those classes and to be responsible for his grades. I pointed out that it would mean we would have to work together to help him achieve success. No more walking away from the responsibility of grades. He agreed.

## COGNITIVE FUNCTION/
## HOMEWORK CHALLENGES

So began a new journey. Our first social studies test was scheduled for the beginning of October. There was a chapter in the book to review but we also had a study guide. Information needing to be memorized was along the lines of geography: knowing continents, oceans, and other geographic terms.

Studying for a test with a child with ADHD can be quite the challenge. This requires executive functioning, the areas where ADHD kids have so much difficulty. According to the National Resource Center on ADHD, a program of CHADD (Children and Adults with ADHD), executive functioning refers "to a wide range of central control processes in the brain that activate, integrate, and manage other brain functions." Components include memory (being able to hold onto facts and pull facts from long-term memory), the ability to get started on something and finish, the ability to control emotions and impulses, and the ability to solve complex problems, which would be multi-stepped.

I could see two areas of executive function that caused stress in the area of preparing for this test. As much as Jon wanted to be a part of the class and receive grades like his classmates, he definitely found it hard to get started. That internal motivation was just not there. In order to get started, he needed me, his external motivator! He also needed the structure of studying each day for a designated period of time. Memorizing of facts does not come easy for him. And of course, his oppositional defiance contributed to his avoidance behavior; that is, in this case, behavior that avoided studying. But the end result of the test better be positive, or in his mind, he was dumb. Result? A lowered self-esteem that only reinforces him not to do work. At least with avoidance, he would not fail. So we studied daily over a few days for this test. The modified test (a word bank) allowed him to do well, a great encouragement for future tests. But he would need to be reminded in the future that he did well and could do well again!

Dr. Thomas Brown, Ph.D., Assistant Clinical Professor of Psychiatry at the Yale University School of Medicine and Associate Director of the Yale Clinic for Attention and Related Disorders, describes six areas of cognitive function. They interact to provide the ability to perform required tasks. They are listed as Activation, Focus, Effort, Emotion, Memory, and Action. He goes further by picking several school-related activities and shows how some of these areas are affected. For instance, in reading comprehension, the executive function of memory is used. Your child may reach a point where he can't remember or recall facts from two pages ago. An area of modification might be: after reading a page or two, going back and asking questions relating to what was just read. This, instead of reading further and allowing the memory to fail, has worked for Jon. Then reading a story becomes less frustrating because you are helping him to grasp and remember main ideas. Why would a child want to struggle through reading when the end result is that he can't remember important facts that hold meaning for the story?

Dr. Brown compares executive function to the conductor of an orchestra. The conductor "organizes, activates, focuses, integrates, and directs the musicians. The brain's executive functions organize, activate, focus, integrate, and direct, allowing the brain to perform both routine and creative work."

Kristin Stanberry, a senior editor/writer for Schwab Learning, wrote about these control processes as another perspective through which we can evaluate a child with learning issues and/or ADHD. Using it as a profile, we can use those different processes; that is, focusing, organizing, self-regulating, using memory, and using effort, to better understand our child with learning issues/ADHD. By doing this, you can better understand areas of weaknesses and areas of strengths. I thought the mention of strengths was very optimistic and refreshing since most of the time, when looking at a child with ADHD and his or her executive function, the assessment is one of negativity. In this case, you are actually looking at both. Once a weakness is found, it can be determined in what way it can be remediated. Once strength is looked at, it can be determined how this strength can possibly be used to compensate for some weaknesses. The other reason I really like this approach is because it puts ADHD in a more visible format. That is, something to grasp, understand, and help.

Kids with ADHD have a medical condition that no one sees. Generally, when no one can see the affliction, it is dismissed if not understood. I am convinced that our world has a long way to go before it understands and accepts ADHD. I think through more education through organizations like CHADD, more people do have more knowledge. The school systems are forced to recognize this diagnosis by law and support it. But the emotional aspect is still there. We know that it exists, and families, teachers, employers, and coaches should embrace it, accept, and deal with it.

But they can't see it; it is a physical affliction that does not affect how a child looks. To many it is abstract and, to many, it is all about misbehaving, being lazy and confrontational, and just plain too busy!! And, of course, it always seems to reflect back on the parents! I have heard parents and teachers (yes) refer to "bad kids." This reference was based on behavior that they believed was not acceptable. How can any kid be bad?

Again, looking at your child's executive functioning profile can help with understanding areas of weaknesses as well as strengths. Modifying areas of weaknesses and using areas of strength to alleviate those weaknesses will serve to improve success in school endeavors.

Even if you can't think of a strength that would directly enhance a weakness, it is still important for your child to know that he has strengths. Knowing this can go a long way in enhancing his self-esteem. At different times, I have tried to make him aware of some of these strengths.

He has always been astutely aware of his environment. I guess that would be known as spatial awareness. Even as a small child, he would know where different landmarks were from his vantage point. He would actually shock me at the ripe old age of 3, when coming from a direction in a car that he was not used to, he would know the direction of his nursery school. Today, once he travels to a place, he knows how to get back! This has been quite useful to many of us, including his siblings! This, of course, always can serve to improve his relationships among his sisters and brother. Can you imagine how good he feels when one of them actually depends on him?

He is also astute in finding people. I can walk onto a crowded baseball field, or walk into a crowded room, and he immediately can find me.

Name a sport or team, and he can tell you who are on it, and all the statistics that go with each player.

He is the most loving and empathetic of his siblings. His demonstrative behavior and verbal expressions show this quite often. Yes, he can be oppositional, but his core spirit is one of love.

Although time factors can be a problem when it comes to the need to start homework or getting ready for bed, when he wants to, he has a keen sense of time as it relates to being somewhere and not being late.

In the area of writing, organizing thoughts and actually initiating the activity are executive functions needed to be successful. I have seen this very frustrating difficulty in Jon. To tell Jon to write sentences using ten spelling words is like telling him to read a four-hundred-page novel in an hour. It is just not going to happen without a lot of intervention. I have learned that because of the significant impairment of this cognitive function, he has a lot of difficulty thinking of and remembering what he wants to say as he writes it down on paper.

To alleviate this, I have written down random words about a topic in order for him to try to organize his thoughts. This way he has a starting point. This would go along with organizing and also getting started, which is another executive function. Until he is more proficient using the key board, I also many times scribe for him. I let him use all of his cognitive energy to come up with an idea and I write as he speaks. This way, he doesn't have a tantrum about the amount of work, and/or end up writing three-word sentences that are not at the level of a fifth grader.

Taking tests requires the usage of the following executive functions: Focusing and Memory. Children with ADHD have poor short-term memory. They also often have difficulty pulling from long-term memory information that is needed. Working memory has also been talked about as being affected in children with ADHD. Working memory is the ability to hold onto facts in order to further figure something out. An example might be a multi-stepped word problem in math. In order for Jon to feel some success in test taking, the tests given need to be modified. For example, fill-in-the-blank sections of a test should be accompanied by word banks. Having a series of words from which to choose to fill in the blanks has definitely promoted his success. In addition, the length of the test should also be modified to allow for improved focus time.

Other modifications can and should include the reading of questions that need to be answered if there is a problem with clarity as well as breaks for increased movement. Increased movement could include standing up and doing jumping jacks. I have actually heard about a teacher allowing a child to bounce on one of those large exercise balls! I don't remember where this happened, but I wish more teachers could be that accommodating!

Actually, Jon's current math teacher allows Jon to stand at his desk while he does his work. For Jon, I am sure this improves his productivity and fulfills the need not to sit still! Certainly, as a side note, I am sure that the acceptance that he feels from his teacher is priceless; a major contribution to success in this class!

Beginning and completing homework within a reasonable amount of time represents the area of executive function that affects actually starting and finishing a project. When Jon comes home from school, he does not want to talk about it or address the need to do homework. I have to admit that this area is quite a struggle. I have dealt with it in varying ways to help accommodate him. I do try to allow for a break: a snack, time for him to ventilate any feelings he has, time for him to go on his computer....but I have found that the most successful avenue is to get started on homework within a reasonable time after school before fatigue sets in and all focus is lost.

There have been times that I have tried to allow for outside play for a half an hour if the weather is nice. He really needs that break to run. I have actually read that being outside among the greenery helps our ADHD children focus. I haven't read a study, but it makes sense, and I have seen it happen. The break for him is really a double-edge sword because his impulsivity and hyperactivity are in full swing... Then to reign him in to focus and do work is very difficult. There are times that he wants to continue to push the envelope and keep playing, especially if there are kids available outside. So this is an area that every parent needs to evaluate in order to best accommodate his or her child.

I think one of the traps that one can fall into with a child with ADHD and learning issues is the enabling trap. That is, you as a mom feel as though it is up to you to ease the transition from school to home. You see that he has had a rough day and is exhausted from all of the energy used to focus and comply with rules. In addition, he knows he is home and can be himself, so to speak. I have been the brunt of countless outbursts of frustration as a result of a challenging day. Examples of this include, "Everyone hates me," "The teacher thinks I am stupid." As you can see, these statements encompass both social and academic components of the day that are difficult. So when the need for homework starts, much anxiety exists as we begin.

He is oppositional many times and feels as if the need to do this homework is an actual attack on him by the teacher. I feel like I am also representing a villain too as I try to encourage the homework completion. He either does not understand the homework, has never been taught the material, or has had a hard day and is too tired to care. So I do enable by staying with him the whole time and help and contribute to answers.

After speaking with his psychologist, Dr. P, I realized that I needed to change my behavior with Jon. I was part of the problem. He suggested that I needed to make him more accountable for this homework. I needed to divide it into parts. I needed to leave the area for a five-minute period while he worked on a piece of the work. After this five-minute period, I should return, make sure things were going well, and leave again for another five-minute period. Previous to this, it would be decided how long this homework would take. At the end of this period, which in this case was thirty minutes, the homework would be over, regardless of whether it was completed.

Dr. P was trying to give Jon the opportunity to own the homework and be responsible. If he refused to do it, then he would lose computer and TV privileges. He would also be responsible for having to face the teacher the next day with unfinished homework. If he did finish the homework in the allotted time, he would lose nothing and would ultimately feel good about the fact that he did the homework independently.

We did follow this suggestion to a degree. Jon did not like the part about having it structured. That is, he did not want me to write this down each day and reward him at the end of the week as Dr. P had suggested. I think that in his mind, it made him be different than other kids. He has never wanted to feel he was being treated differently, even though in reality he is. We are still working on this.

I have not divided up the homework into sections. But I have left him for brief periods so that he can feel accomplished and responsible for this work. There has been some improvement in his oppositional behavior. It is a work in progress, though. But Dr. P is very passionate about this being necessary to encourage a positive relationship with Jon and me. He feels that it is imperative that I encourage independence. The dependent relationship is unhealthy for everyone. I think sometimes that we as parents do not realize the mistakes we make. We think that what we are doing is easing their frustration and pain of the day, but we are only encouraging dependence and anger.

What is best for the child with ADHD is a consistent pattern of doing things. Without that, disorganization ensues, and because yesterday Jon was able to avoid homework until six p.m., then he will certainly try to avoid it again the next day. Breaks are great after school, but it's important to stay on the same time frame. Jon needs to know that at four p.m. homework will begin. If there is a change to be made in the daily after school schedule for any reason, then formulate in your head how much variation you will allow, and tell your child what the new schedule will be ahead of time. This is important because many times the initiation of the activity is the area of executive function that is hampered.

I found it interesting that many times Jon would be very concerned about doing well on a test, but that without setting up of the homework schedule he would do no studying at all...meaning that executive function of activation was truly affected. Within this previous discussion, as you can see, sense of time was also adversely affected in a child with ADHD. That comes up in many areas, but I have found it to be most prevalent in this area of homework.

The area of control of emotion is also affected by ADHD, and is a part of executive function. This can also be seen in the area of doing homework. Anger, frustration, and a lowered sense of self-esteem are very evident some days after school prior to and as homework is started. Before something is even looked at, Jon can tell me that he doesn't understand it. Of course, this information has been discussed in school and should be a review. I think sometimes he is actually afraid that he will have forgotten what he needs to know, or there will be areas that he never really understood. In his mind, it is easier to give up.

I have found it such a trying time, but it is important to react in a way that helps to continue to encourage ability and an elevated self-esteem. I sit next to him and encourage him to start from the beginning and read the directions. I am always telling him that I am here to help and support but to not do it for him. Sometimes he is confused by the directions and I have to put them in different words...or visually show him by doing the first problem, whether it be math or a language paper, always trying to put forth the attitude that I believe he is capable, despite his confusion.

Recently Jon told me that he could not do two of the math problems for homework. They happened to be word problems dealing with fractions, just like previous problems. I made him read aloud those problems and he then, without assistance, was able to give the correct answer. I told him I was proud of him and that I did not understand why he would say he could not do it. He responded that the words looked confusing. So I guess in this case many things came into play: his inability to focus at the end of a long day, his dyslexia, and his fear that he could not read the passage because of his past difficulties. He stopped short of trying and gave up on himself! It was easier to avoid rather than experience another failure in his mind.

That was quite a learning curve for me. I needed to continue to encourage him to be independent and celebrate the successes! And of course this was important in school too.

In addition, I modify homework if necessary. This is important in order to stay within the time allotment for homework as was stated previously. This ability should be spelled out in your child's IEP to avoid any confusion. If the directions state to re-write a sentence with the correct verb, I allow Jon to re-write the verb only. The important piece is to at least make him read the sentence, not just plug the word in. This way, you as the parent can be sure that he can read the sentence and that the verb chosen sounds right to him.

I remember going to a CHADD meeting last year. A mom who was there stated that she rarely went to evening meetings. Many times she and her son were doing homework until nine p.m. That is absolutely horrendous! In children without any issues, homework is supposed to be no longer than ten minutes per grade level, which means Jon should take no longer than fifty minutes to do his homework because he is in fifth grade. Any longer and there should be more modification.

Another area of executive function is the ability to analyze, pull apart, and figure out a problem, using multi-steps. I know this will come into play as Jon grows older and is expected to do projects, long-term reports, and group work. But on a smaller level, I see a child who has difficulty in a math problem filtering out the data that is not needed. Teaching him to help himself in analyzing a problem, I think, includes the necessity to either highlight important facts or cross out facts not pertinent to figuring out the problem. This is a very systematic approach, but again an area where it is hard to get started.

A recent example of this was an assigned project regarding colonial times. Jon chose to do jobs in those times and told his resource room teacher that he would do a PowerPoint presentation. His aide told me about this one time when I was in the building in the library where Jon was looking up information. I was nervous because, although they told me that he knew about PowerPoint presentations because he had done a couple of them in the resource room, I was not confident that he could do this independently.

I was right. I think he understood the basics of PowerPoint. But what he fell short on was the ability to go through books and pull the information that was needed. Organizational skills are needed to do such a project. I really don't think that his resource room teacher and aide took that into account when discussing this project. He needed help in that area, help that he received from me, since there was apparently little time to do this project in school. It was also apparent that there was a serious lack of teacher knowledge regarding how areas of executive function can adversely affect the successful completion of a project.

Organization is an area which I consistently hear is problematic for kids with ADHD. There is so much support needed in the early grades to hopefully learn as time goes by how to compensate for this deficit. Obviously, in the early grades, an assignment book is important. Here, requirements for every subject can be written down. As children get older, they have to deal with multiple teachers and, of course, multiple expectations. Binders with dividers and folders are all part of keeping the ADHD child organized. In addition, a buddy might be helpful in the area of remembering what to bring home from his locker at the end of a day.

The use of technology has been suggested to me as Jon gets older to facilitate his academic success. Taping lectures and using books with tapes would certainly help.

All of the issues of executive functioning can hinder academic success in a child with ADHD. It is so important to continue to monitor those needs as the child grows. Accommodations where necessary can mean stronger self-esteem and a reason to work hard and succeed.

## AFFIRMATION OF POSITIVE OUTCOMES
## TO MEDICATION

Something happened recently that somewhat alleviated my ongoing stress related to medicating my son and is somewhat of a reinforcement of medication support in some of our ADHD children. His resource room teacher called at the end of the day to ask me if there was anything different in Jon's life; was there anything that caused him to be upset at home? Her reason for asking had to do with behavior noted that day. Jon was impulsive, blurting out answers, and disruptive. I could not believe it!! He had an issue that morning while taking his medication. He takes a multivitamin as well as Focalin. He had been in a rush since, in his head, he needs to be at the bus stop (the end of our driveway) at precisely 7:57 a.m. (Yes, here is an example of being very cognizant of time in order to be first at the bus stop!) He was running thirty seconds behind schedule, necessitating a major rush during swallowing his pill. At one point, I looked at him and saw a pink face, with pink liquid falling from his mouth!! As he left, I saw a piece of capsule from his medication! So obviously he had lost part of his multivitamin and some of his medication in his mad dash to the door!

I did not feel comfortable re-medicating him since I just could not be sure how much he had lost. As a result of the phone call it became obvious that he had lost a great deal! He could not control his impulses. Ms. D told me that it was obvious that he was working at trying to control himself, but many times he was unsuccessful. He obsessed over things from which he normally would recover. Obsessions that the teacher mentioned included worrying about time to get things done. Impulsivity included yelling out answers and interrupting. (This of course I see all the time, since by the time he comes home the medication has been metabolized.) The kids in his class apparently seemed stunned and looked back and forth from him to his teacher in amazement. But they fortunately stopped short of making fun of him.

Medication does not change the individual. But it does make it possible for this ADHD child to work on impulse control, obsess less on issues of concern, and be more socially aware. By socially, I mean the ability to make jokes, laugh at oneself, understand body language, and respect others. In short, it allows for the ability to knowingly do the right things. As per Dr. Brown, it is not the lack of knowledge but the inability to act out that knowledge.

Again there was a time when I was horrified at the thought of giving my child stimulants. Now, like back in the beginning of first grade, I thanked God that medication exists as a form of therapy for my son. For him, it is as important as insulin is to a diabetic. The statistics show how an untreated ADHD child is much more likely to abuse drugs and alcohol. It makes so much sense! Can you imagine a child like mine going through the school system untreated? As his self-esteem plummeted, why wouldn't he choose the path of self-medicating as a source of comfort? And who knows what he would use to sooth himself?

There is no doubt in my mind that Jon was well aware of the unacceptable behavior that day…and of the scrutiny that surrounded him. Children with ADHD are intelligent and sensitive. I mentioned his day when he came home; that the teacher had called and told me that he had had a rough day .He obviously did not want to talk about it. He said, yeah, and then ran outside to let off steam. I could not push any more conversation. I would in the future when we were both ready. But he could not talk about it just then, and, for some reason, I just knew that I had to respect his wishes for now.

I think it has always been hard for him to accept taking medication. He has always said that he just wants to be like other kids and not take medication. Now I think this day at school served as a source of information for him. He discovered how much that medication was helping him to stay focused and less impulsive.

## ADHD AND THE FAMILY

Although much of what I have talked about deals with school and modifications, it would be remiss of me if I did not touch on the home life. When a family has a child with ADHD, the whole family must deal with that invisible diagnosis in a positive way to remain healthy. It certainly is easy to say, hard at times to do. It is hard when a family is watching football and the child with ADHD is running and throwing a football. When an older sibling is talking, this child may feel that he is not involved with the group and then proceeds to interrupt and talk excessively. Attention is important to Jon, as with others with ADHD. Even if the attention is gotten through negative means, that's ok with him. He merely reacts with his uncontrolled emotion, which is also a part of a deficit of executive function.

It is not only important to understand ADHD within the family but also imperative I think to beable to look at it in a positive way. Reinforcing that ADHD is not a disorder but a gift in many ways would enforce a positive way at looking at the child by the rest of the family.

It's difficult too when his twenty-year-old brother is his basketball coach. Showing attention to others on the team can be misconstrued by Jon as Justin believing others are better than he is at the sport. Of course, without issues, this would be difficult enough since a younger brother generally will look up to the older one. Feelings of insecurity, along with lack of impulse control and emotional regulation, can certainly contribute to a tumultuous relationship.

But despite all of that, I think through Justin coaching basketball there has been a strengthening of the relationship. Again, here is another strength. Jon has the speed and ability in basketball that Justin never had. He himself has said this to me. I do think he admires this in Jon, which of course can only make Jon feel so much better about himself.

Parental relationships can be certainly tested at times. It is important not to take emotional outbursts personally. We as parents are responsible for the daily structure of this child. The frustrations of the day come home at three p.m. According to Jon, it is my fault many times that he has homework, that he did not understand many things during the day, that he feels stupid, that he thinks his teacher and peers think he's stupid, and that he plain just doesn't feel accepted many times throughout the day. There have been times that he has expressed hate to both of us…It is hard to accept that and not take it personally.

It is important not to take that kind of emotional outburst seriously. Emotional control is a struggle for children with ADHD. I have found that it is important to remain calm. Any outbursts that occur because I am upset only fuel his anger, frustration, and self-deprecation. It is not easy and I have made so many mistakes… and will continue to make them. But try to keep in mind to either try to redirect anger or possibly walk away until things are calmer.

I think it's ok for a child to know that sometimes, as a human being like him, we as parents can not handle these verbal attacks. Rather than attack back, it is better to go to a quiet place until he calms down and things can be talked about rationally. This also serves as modeling for good behavior and keeps relationships intact.

Sometimes it is good for families to seek behavioral therapists to enlist help in handling difficult situations. But I also think that the more information that you have regarding ADHD, the more you can understand certain behaviors and react accordingly.

Sometimes adversities and difficult times cause us to ask the question "why?" .How can all of this be put into perspective? I asked how I could find meaning in having a child with ADHD as I also struggled to understand him and accept him.

# CHADD/PARENT2PARENT INFORMATION

CHADD, Children and Adults with ADHD, is an organization that has been in existence for twenty years. It is informational and supportive for families dealing with ADHD. A program was put together in order to offer people the option to become certified to reach out to others struggling with this diagnosis. Parent2parent training is offered throughout the country to those who are interested. Once you are certified, it is your responsibility to offer a series of seven informational classes, two hours in length, to families in your community. As a result of the common denominator of ADHD, it also in many ways becomes a support group.

I remember how I felt when Jon was six and just diagnosed with ADHD. Although it was the beginning of a long journey, it was also the beginning of a very different upbringing for a very special child with gifts that would not be immediately seen by his world and certainly not by many school personnel...The first learning consultant telling us of the necessity of medication, to which Vince and I were adamantly opposed, and then the school telling us weeks later that our son not only was on the wrong page during class but in the wrong book! He was a child who was always looking out of the window and not engaged with the rest of the class; a child who was alienating his peers by pushing through personal space, interrupting, and arguing; a child whose self-esteem was spiraling downward.

I decided to take the opportunity to travel to Pennsylvania and take this two-and-a-half-day class to learn...and also to become certified in order to reach out to other families in need. I wish there had been a certified teacher to go to when Jon was newly diagnosed to better understand and advocate for him.

I am currently the only parent 2parent teacher in south jersey. CHADD sponsors this certification but does not endorse any of the content of the personal journey found in this book, medications, learning consultants, or reading programs. CHADD offers information and support. My second set of classes is finishing up in a couple of weeks. Each participant receives a binder full of articles so that one can always refer back to different areas when needed. Participants can feel comfort in the knowledge they receive: a medical diagnosis that shows us reason for behavior and how this behavior can be changed. They can also receive support in a group that is going through the same things and understands them.

Knowledge and support are needed to teach and advocate for the child with ADHD, a child who, in the school environment, is sometimes like a round peg forced into a square hole, a child with gifts that no one can see.

Families like us have a long journey as we support and advocate for our children with ADHD. But it is important to realize that we are their best advocates. We can not be alienated or intimidated by those who are academic professionals. Anyone who becomes knowledgeable about ADHD can advocate for the needs of their children successfully. If not us, then who will pick them up during this long journey as they stumble and fall? We as parents know that, although the disability is invisible to those who don't understand, we are their cornerstone. It is imperative that we continue to support them in their world, educate those who impact their lives, and ensure that they understand themselves so that they too can have the self-esteem to stand tall in this often very difficult, intolerant world.

In addition to the above, try to retain a sense of humor....imagine a child who watches a baseball game, throwing a ball, and pretending to swing a bat throughout the entire game! My husband quipped: Jon only sits during the seventh inning stretch! How true...The Seventh Inning Sit.

# REFERENCES

ADDitude Ed.,"ADHD at School: Hyperactivity Help Strategies for Harnessing ADHD Hyperactivity in the Classroom." http:// www.ADDitudemag.com.

Arnold,Eugene L.,M.D.,et. al. "Understanding the 36 Month MTA Follow-Up Findings in Context." Attention Apr.2008: 14-18.

Barkley,Russell,PhD. Taking Charge of ADHD. Guilford Press, 2000.

Barkley,Russell,PhD., and Christine Benton. Your Defiant Child. New York: The Guilford Press,1998.

Barkley, Russell,PhD. "Excerpts From a Lecture in San Francisco, Ca. 17 June 2000." http://www.Schwab Learning.org

Brown,Thomas,PhD. "ADHD and Co-Occurring Conditions." Attention Feb.2009: 10-15.

Brown,Thomas,PhD. "Executive Functions: Describing Six Aspects of a Complex Syndrome." Attention Feb.2008: 12-17.

Cooper-Kahn, Joyce,PhD.,and Laurie Dietzel,PhD. "Helping Children with Executive Functioning." Attention Feb.2009: 17-21.

www.Chadd.org, Children and Adults with Attention-Deficit Hyperactivity Disorder.

Hallowell,Ned,M.D., Podcast: "ADD is a Gift."
http://www.ADDitudemag.com.

Hallowell,Ned,M.D., Podcast: "A Plan for Living with ADD."
http://www.ADDitudemag.com.

Hallowell,Ned,M.D., Podcast: "Medication."
http://www.ADDitudemag.com.

www.Help4adhd.org: National Resource Center on ADHD, A
Program of CHADD.

Howey,Pat,Paralegal and Advocate. "What You Need to Know
About IDEA 2004: Present Levels of Functional
Performance and Functional Goals in IEPs." 1998-2008.
http://www.Wrightslaw.com/howey/iep.functional.perf.htm.

Rothman,Jean. Medically reviewed by Kevin O. Hwang,M.D.,MPH.
"How Exercise Helps With ADHD Symptoms." 20 Mar. 2009.
http://www.everydayhealth.com/health-report/

Shaywitz,Sally,M.D. Overcoming Dyslexia. New York: Vintage
Books, A Division of Random House, Inc., 2003.

Smith,Linda, Beth Kaplanek, Mary Durheim, and Terry Illes. Parent-
to-Parent Family Training on ADHD. Funded by the CHADD
President's Council, CHADD Parent to Parent 2008.

Stanberry,Kristen. "Executive Function: A New Lens Through
Which to View Your Child." 22 Oct. 2007.
http://www.Schwablearning.org.

Stanberry, Kristen. "Assistive Technology for Kids with Learning Disabilities-An Overview." March 2009. http://www.greatschools.net.

Stanberry,Kristen. "Defining Dyslexia: A Modern Dilemma." April 2003. http://www.greatschools.net.

Steedman,Wayne,Esq.,"10 Tips: How to Use IDEA 2004 to Improve Your Child's Special Education." 1998-2008. http://www.wrightslaw.com/idea/art/10.tips.steedman.htm.

Taylor,Andrea Faber and Frances E. Kuo. "Children with Attention Deficits Concentrate Better After Walk In the Park." 6 Mar. 2009. Http://www.myadhd.com.

The International Dyslexia Association. http://www.interdys.org/What we do.htm

Wright,Peter,esq. and Pam Wright. "Who is Eligible for Protections Under Section 504 but Not Under IDEA?" 1998-2008. http://www.wrightslaw.com/info/sec504.who.protect.htm.

Wright,Peter,esq. and Pam Wright. "Roadmap to IEPS: Highly Qualified Teachers and Research Based Instruction." 1998-2008. http://www.wrightslaw.com/idea/art/ieps.rbi.htm.

Wright,Peter,esg. and Pam Wright. "Reading at Wrightslaw." 1998-2008. http://www.wrightslaw.com/info/Read.index.htm.

Made in the USA
Charleston, SC
16 February 2010